GW00642556

The
WYE VALLEY
RAILWAY

by
Brian M. Handley

THE OAKWOOD PRESS

© Oakwood Press 1988

First published 1982

ISBN 0 85361 283 8

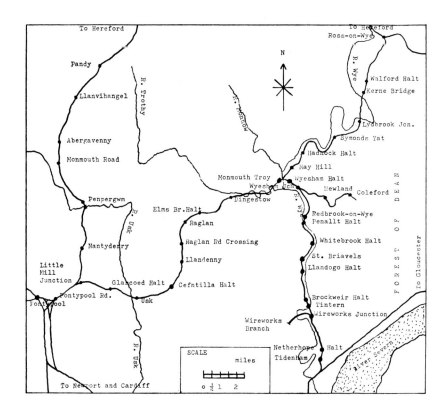

Published by The OAKWOOD PRESS, P.O.Box 122, Headington, Oxford.

THE Wye Valley is an area of outstanding natural beauty and great historical interest and through its pleasant pastures flows one of the most famous rivers in Great Britain, the Wye. The river rises in Powys on Plinlimon and flows south on into England, where passing through Herefordshire it separates that country from Wales. The Wye stretches for one hundred and thirty miles before entering the estuary of the Severn at Chepstow and during its course it passes through the rural counties of Herefordishire and Gwent where its tributories the Elan, Lugg and Monnow are received.

Its name was derived from the medieval spelling Waie and the river was of paramount importance to Monmouth, it was the vital artery that supplied the town with the bulk of its trade and in turn allowed Monmouth to send its goods world wide. Before electricity the tributories of the Wye supplied power to drive the machinery in the wood processing and iron producing centres situated along the river.

Besides its natural beauty the Wye Valley has important historical buildings and many archaelogical sites, possibly the most famous of its treasured monuments is Tintern Abbey. Built in 1131 by the Cistercian Monks, it was once one of the wealthiest Cistercian houses in England.

In contrast to the Abbey the mammoth fortification of Offas Dyke has few obvious remains. Between Chepstow and Monmouth the Dyke follows close to the river and once formed the boundary between Mercia and the Welsh. It was built by King Offa about 779 B.C. and carved a trench through three English and four Welsh Counties.

The lower regions of the Wye Valley, south of Monmouth was for a long time the main iron producing area of Britain, this was due largely to the industrious influence of the Cistercian monastic order, coupled with the fact that there was an abundant supply of fuel for the furnaces and readily available water power for the forges. The importance of the iron became widely realised in the 13th Century and output increased rapidly at the Wyeside forges, principally at Tintern, where the first wire mills in Britain to be operated by water power were established in 1566. Soon afterwards, a furnace was built near Tintern to manufacture the "Osmond Iron" necessary to produce the finest wire. Almost three hundred years later wire produced here was used in the first transatlantic telegraph cable laid by Sir Daniel Gooch (who was the first Chief Mechanical Engineer and later Chairman of the Great Western Railway). It was also at Tintern in 1568 that brass was made for the first time in Britain.

Prior to the coming of the railways, the majority of Monmouth's trade was based on the river with merchandise being despatched down the Wye to Chepstow, Monmouth's nearest seaport and then onto the larger ports of Cardiff, Newport and Bristol. Although trade had continued in this fashion for many centuries, as industry along the Wye increased it was not altogether successful as the Wye was navigable only as far as Brockweir for vessels of 80/90 tons after this point the cargo had to be separated into smaller units and loaded onto shallow draft barges, known as trows which were suited to the shallow waters up river to Monmouth. This break in shipment was costly in time and money for the manufacturing industries along the Wye Valley. Consequently with this need for a more efficient form of transport and the age of romantic tourism about to dawn, the 1850's saw the arrival of Monmouth's long awaited link to the national railway system.

A brief survey of the railways in the area will set the scene for the history of the Wye Valley Railway itself.

The Coleford, Monmouth Usk and Pontypool Railway

As with most other parts of the country during this period of railway expansion, many fanciful schemes were proposed to run to or through the historic town of Monmouth, none of which materialised until early in October, 1857 the Coleford, Monmouth Usk and Pontypool Railway became the first to reach the then county town (Monmouth relinquished the title in 1939, Newport now has this distinction). The railway was intended to eventually link up with a tramroad known as the "Monmouth Railway" at Wyesham on the east bank of the river just opposite the town of Monmouth, consequently allowing the C.M.U.P.R. access to the rich timber and coal assets of the Forest of Dean.

The C.M.U.P.R. was authorised by an Act of Parliament on 20th August, 1853, allowing the company to construct a railway from Little Mill Junction on the then Newport, Abergavenny and Hereford Railway about two miles north of Pontypool Road Station to Coleford with a branch at Dixton giving access to Monmouth Gas Works. The section from Little Mill to Usk was the first to be opened on the 2nd June, 1856 and was worked by the N.A. and H. Railway until the 12th October, 1857, this being the date of the completion of the line into Monmouth and the opening of Troy Station.

When the C.M.U.P.R. commenced service, passenger and freight trains were operated between Little Mill Junction and Monmouth Troy with the intermediate stations situated at Usk, Llandenny, Raglan Road and Dingestow. But like many country branches, stops were also made where necessary and this became a regular practice at a place known as Raglan Footpath. The reason for this was that the official station was situated someway out of Raglan but as the name "Footpath" suggests, there was no road connection.

On the 1st July, 1861 the C.M.U.P.R. was leased to a concern known as the West Midlands Railway Company which had been formed by an Act of Parliament on the 14th June, 1860. This company under the Chairmanship of William Fenton involved the amalgamation of the Newport, Abergavenny and Hereford Railway, the Worcester and Hereford Railway and the Oxford, Worcester and Wolverhampton Railway (The Old Worse and Worse).

The time of leasing was significant as it was the date of the first closure on the line at Little Mill Junction Station after which services had run to and from Pontypool Road. However, in 1863 the station was re-opened.

The halts and stations along the old C.M.U.P.R. route remained the same until 1876 when under the G.W.R. control Raglan Station was officially transferred to the one time unofficial stopping place known as Raglan Footpath. The original Raglan Station was closed to be later re-opened as a Halt on the 24th July, 1931. Three more Halts were subsequently added, the first in 1927 at Glascoed between Little Mill and Usk, Elm Bridge Halt was next situated between Raglan and Dingestow and opened on the 27th November, 1933 and the final halt was Cefntilla opened on the 14th June, 1954 between Llandenny and Usk.

During 1861 while under W.M.R. control a short stretch of line was opened across the Wye at Wyesham via a magnificent stone viaduct and iron bridge, thus enabling the C.M.U.P.R. to fulfill its original plan of reaching the Forest of Dean and taking advantage of its natural resources, the 1853 Act had inpowered the C.M.U.P.R. to purchase the Monmouth Railway Companies undertakings which consisted of two routes between Monmouth and Coleford. Unfortunately due to its leasing to the W.M.R. and eventual amalgamation with the Great Western Railway on the 1st July, 1863, these options were never taken up, in fact construction of the Pontypool to Coleford Railway stopped short at Monmouth Troy Station for passenger traffic and at Wyesham for goods.

The Ross and Monmouth Railway

Eight years after the arrival of the C.M.U.P.R. a second railway company was to drive its metals towards Monmouth, this was the Ross and Monmouth Railway authorised by an Act of Parliament on the 5th July, 1865, it took eight years to build and was worked from its inception by the Great Western Railway, the contractor was Joseph Firbank, the line was first opened to passenger traffic on the 4th August, 1873.

The station at Monmouth was situated at Mayhill on the east bank of the Wye and was initially a terminal station, as the bridge over the river (which still survives) was not completed for several months after the opening ceremony. On completion of the bridge the line was extended over the river to Monmouth Troy Station and was opened to traffic on the 1st May, 1874.

There were five stopping places erected along the twelve and a half mile route, these included three stations which were built during the initial construction of the line, they were situated at Kerne Bridge, Lydbrook Junction and Symonds Yat, and two halts which were added later, the first at Walford which was opened in April, 1931 and a second at Hadnock opened as late as June, 1951. The Ross and Monmouth was the only one of Monmouth's Railways to remain independent until the 1921 Railways Act forced its amalgamation with G.W.R. in 1922.

The Coleford Railway

The shortest lived standard gauge railway in the lower regions of the Wye Valley was the G.W.R. branch known as the Coleford Railway. It was opened from Wyesham Junction to Coleford on the 1st September, 1883 and was owned and built by the Coleford Railway Company and worked by the Great Western Railway from the opening date. The G.W.R. took over the company entirely in 1884 (47 and 48 Vict. Cap. 235).

The Coleford Railway was the fourth branch line to run from Monmouth Troy Station and was intended to take advantage of the Forest of Dean's natural resources, i.e., coal and timber, the objective that the Coleford, Monmouth Usk and Pontypool Railway had failed to reach. The line ran from Wyesham Junction to Coleford in the Forest of Dean superceding the old Coleford Tramway which had run from Mayhill to Coleford and was originally called the Monmouth Railway when opened in 1813. Stations on the new line were built at Newlands and Coleford.

From Monmouth to Coleford the line ascended 500 feet over a distance of six miles, rising all the way on a gradient which varied from 1 in 40 to 1 in 105, the greater portion being between 1 in 40 and 1 in 67. The line was worked by ordinary staff and ticket and auxiliary block telegraph under the standard regulations. The maximum speed permitted over any part of the branch was 20 miles per hour, but a special restriction of 15 m.p.h. was imposed over the facing points at Newlands Whitecliff sidings and Coleford and of 5 m.p.h. through Wyesham Junction, where all down goods trains had to stop dead on the loop.

Throughout its operating life the line never really fulfilled the hopes expected of it and it was closed on New Year's Day, 1917. Shortly afterwards most of the track was lifted and the rails were shipped to Flanders to support the war effort. The only exception was just over a mile of track including the passing loops, telegraph poles and signal box at Wyesham, but not the signals. These remained in situ for twelve years after the closure and were finally removed in July, 1929.

After railway operations had ceased, the tunnel at Newlands was taken over for the cultivation of mushrooms and during the Second World War, Newland Station was requisitioned by the Air Ministry as their local headquarters with the signal box becoming the guard-room. In connection with this military presence at Newlands the two tunnels at Redbrook were used as ammunition stores after the ends of both structures had been bricked up.

The Coleford Branch was the first of Monmouth's Standard Gauge steam railways to be closed. The C.M.U.P.R. lingered on for just over a quarter of a century. But it was destined to follow the example of the Coleford Branch. The last train to run over the Coleford, Monmouth Usk and Pontypool Railway between Pontypool and Monmouth Troy Station was a Stephenson Locomotive Society Special, which ironically ran on the Railways Centenary date, the 12th October, 1957. Dismantling of the line commenced soon afterwards in September, 1957. Sadly within less than eighteen months the Ross and Monmouth Railway followed the course of its two predecessors, when in January, 1959 it was served with a closure notice, consequently its passenger service was withdrawn, although goods and freight services continued for a further five years until the inevitable final closure of the line in January, 1964.

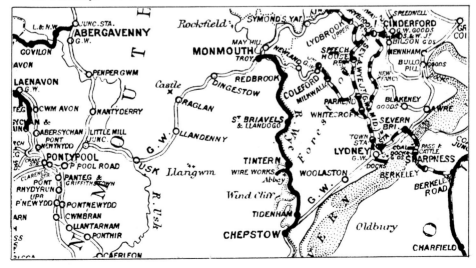

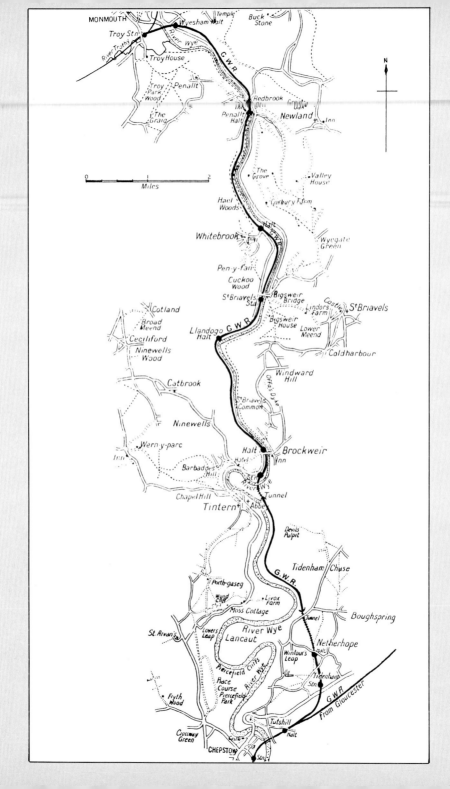

The abolition of Monmouth's railways was almost complete. The town's brief courtship with the permanent way had almost drawn to a close, but surely the most romantic affair must have been with the picturesque Wye Valley Railway, of which a short stretch at the southern end known as the Tintern Branch, is still in use today. Ballast trains running to and from Tintern Quarry makes it the only working survivor of Monmouth's four railways.

There were several sound commercial reasons for promoting a railway between Monmouth and Chepstow, the most obvious was to capitalise on the freight and passenger trade that needed to travel between the two towns. Prior to the opening of the Wye Valley Railway the Victorian traveller or businessman had certainly experienced the great way round, as the only link by rail was to travel in a south westerly direction on the Coleford, Monmouth Usk and Pontypool Railway and then go via Pontypool and Newport to reach Chepstow making a journey of some forty-three miles. The new line proposed a direct route shortening the distance to fifteen miles. By reducing the distance to Chepstow this consequently made access to Bristol all the more easier. The advantage to commerce, industry and the travelling public was obvious. It was also evident that the railway was a popular and welcomed venture with the local communities along the Wye Valley as the following extract from the Monmouthshire Beacon reported.

> " Whilst opening up a new district hitherto unapproached by railway traffic, the new line will prove a great convenience not only to the locality through which it runs, but to the travelling public at large and in point of time it will shorten the journey to Bristol by two hours."

> (Monmouthshire Beacon 1876)
> 21.10.1876

The promoters already realised the potential of the Severn Tunnel project and the possibility that the Wye Valley line could play a major role in carrying through traffic from Bristol to the North of England and vice versa. "The gradients and curves of the line are good, the line having been constructed with the idea of accommodating the through traffic from Bristol to the North of England." (Monmouthshire Beacon 1876).

> "Statement of gross traffic per annum £36,779 does not include any estimate of revenue received by traffic passing over the line on completion of the Severn Tunnel now being constructed." (S. H. Yockney, F.G.S., M.Inst.C.E.), 24.3.1874.

The proposed railway would also be a prime factor in the development of Chepstow as a port receiving merchandise direct instead of playing second fiddle to Swansea, Cardiff and Newport. "The port of Chepstow at the south end of the line may now by means of this new railway become a competing port." (Illustrated London News, October, 1876).

Another very important but seasonal source of revenue was to be expected from the ever increasing tourist trade encouraged by the beauty of the Wye Valley area. For the Victorian sightseer the new line would provide superb views of the Wye Valley and its surrounding countryside, an exclusive panorama to be observed at will, from the armchair comfort of the railway carriage.

The necessity for a railway had to be proved before public money could be found, or Parliament persuaded to give the necessary authority but with such a wealth of positive research to back the project the promoters confidently presented their plans before Parliament.

Plans were first drawn up for a railway to run between Chepstow and Monmouth in 1865 (deposited plans for Wye Valley Railway 1865). It was proposed that the line should run along the Welsh West Bank of the river; this would of meant that the railway would have passed through Tintern village and not around it, as eventually happened. However, this plan was revised the following year, and the line was re-routed along the East Bank. The revised Wye Valley Railway Bill was presented before a Select Committee of the House of Lords on 13th July, 1866; the proceedings were chaired by the Earl of Romeny and Mr. Mereweather heard the opening case for the Promoters. Mr. Charles Baker a Solicitor, acting for the Duke of Beaufort was questioned by Mr. Cripps and Mr. Grenville Somerset, Queen's Councillors acting on behalf of the Parliamentary Committee. On cross examination Mr. Baker reported that two thirds of the land required by the railway belonged to the Duke of Beaufort; this consisted of some eight to ten miles of the total route mileage. It transpired that there was no problem in acquiring this necessary land as the Duke of Beaufort was in complete favour of the railway. An objection was brought about by the Parliamentary Committee regarding damage to the ancient site of Tintern Abbey. It was stated that the proposed line was to bring no injury to any part of the Abbey, land or buildings. Mr. Baker replied that there would be no danger to the Abbey or its surrounding boundaries.

The cross examination then continued with Lieutenant Colonel Willoughby S. Rook of the Scots Fusiliers Guards and Magistrate for Monmouth. Mr. Rook was also owner of the Bigsweir and Kynaston Estates which were situated part in Gloucestershire and part in Monmouthshire. Along with the Duke of Beaufort's the Lt. Col.'s was all the property that was proposed to be taken by the Wye Valley Railway Company. Mr. Rook had no objection to the railway. When questioned about his preference of gauge i.e., the Stephenson Gauge of 4' 8½" or the Brunel Gauge of 7' 0¼", he was impartial to whatever gauge was to be used. His uncommital reply was most likely due to the fact that he was unaware of the importance attached to the choice of gauge. Had the 7' 0¼" broad gauge been used it would have certainly caused problems at Wyesham, situated at the northern end of the line and the Wye Valley Junction at the southern end, as these two places operated on the Standard Gauge. (This gauge was also referred to rather mockingly by Brunel as the Colliers Gauge).

This break of gauge situation had occurred not far from the Wye Valley at Gloucester in the early 1840's where the Bristol and Gloucester Railway (Broad gauge) had met the Birmingham and Gloucester Railway (Standard gauge); the annoyance and aggrevation caused here brought the whole question of gauge to a head and eventually did much to bring about Parliamentary intervention. A three man committee was formed known as the gauge commission consisting of Lieutenant Colonel Sir Frederick Smith, first Inspector General of Railways of the Board of Trade. George Riddell Airy, Astronomer Royal and Peter Barlow Professor of Mathematics at the Royal Military Academy, Woolwich. After close scrutiny of the railway gauge situation the Committee decided in favour of Stephenson Gauge. This was made official by the Gauges Act of 1846 which forbad the construction of non-Standard gauge railways, but made an exception for extensions to existing broad gauge railways situated mainly in the West Country.

The Act was really the final blow to Brunels much loved Broad gauge. The first Broad gauge to Standard gauge conversion took place near Monmouth on a twenty-two and a half mile stretch of line between Grange Court and Hereford on the Hereford, Ross and Gloucester Railway in 1869.

There had been some opposition to the Wye Valley Railway Bill on its initial reading because of the proposed Broad gauge construction but the opposition was dropped when it was confirmed that Standard gauge track was to be used. When the question of land and gauge had been successfully debated the Committee then moved to the next stage, that of engineering and estimated cost of construction. Mr. William Henry Lefevre (Civil Engineer) was working on the project in conjunction with S. H. Yockney & Son of Westminster, who were the official Engineers, and had carried out the initial survey. Mr. Lefevre reported that the estimated cost had been set at £222,298 for fourteen and a half miles of line from the G.W.R. Junction known as the Wye Valley Junction to Monmouth, and that the steepest gradient would be 1 in 71 for six furlongs. Two tunnels were to be built, one estimated to be two hundred and forty-nine yards and the other an estimated length of seven hundred and fifteen yards.

On completion, the line had cost a little over £318,000 the largest part of the budget being spent on the construction of Tidenham Tunnel.

The Wye Valley Railway Bill managed to get a successful reading and Parliament sanctioned the line on the 10th August, 1866. It was incorporated under the Wye Valley Railway Act (29 and 30 Vict. Cap. CCCLVIII) and (34.35 Vict. Cap. XLLX) with a share capital of £230,000 and the usual borrowing powers. The Railway had now all the powers necessary to commence building, but construction did not begin for another eight years; this delay must have been influenced by the prevailing financial situation evident in the country at that time. In 1866 the bubble had burst on the last of the country's railway manias. The railway investment fever had started early in the decade, people and companies speculated their life savings and investments in fanciful railway schemes, in the hope of getting rich quick. But like previous manias these speculative ventures were to come to nothing, leaving the investors destitute and bankrupt. The outcome of these exploits was one of the worst financial crashes of the century. Subsequently it became obvious that some source of Government intervention would be needed to prevent a reoccurrence of these events. This led to the (Railway Companies Act 1867) which imposed stricter financial control and as a result tightened the reins on railway promoting.

The first Board of Directors indeed the original promoters of the Wye Valley Railway Company consisted of five people led by the Chairman, Mr. William Hawes, Esq., F.G.S., who was also a trustee of the Company. He was no newcomer to the business of railway promoting as he was also the Chairman of a modest railway in the south of England known as the East London Railway Company which was incorporated in 1865 to take over and convert a tunnel that ran under the River Thames between Rotherhithe and Wapping. There were several similarities between the East London Railway and the Wye Valley Railway; for example neither company ever owned locomotives or rolling stock and both companies had board-room difficulties. It was also true to say that neither companies prospered and both formed what could be called a useful North-South connection.

The second railway personality on the Board was Lord Alexander Gordon Lennox. He would have already experienced Hawes' board-room manner as he was also a Director of the London, Brighton and South Coast Railway which worked and operated Hawes' East London Railway. The three remaining Directors were Mr. Hew Dalrymple, Esq., Trustee of the W.V.R. and Director of the Bristol Port and Channel Dock Company, Clifton. Mr. Isaac W. Home, Esq., Director of the Bridgefield and Victoria Company Ltd., London and finally

Mr. James Goodson, Esq., who was the third trustee and also Chairman of the Guardian Fire and Life Assurance Company.

It will be noted that a local connection as was common with many other country branches did not exist between the Board of Directors and the W.V.R. The Board members were purely business entrepreneurs led by the Chairman, Mr. Hawes, who had seen an opportunity to make money, by speculating on a railway that for the most part would operate as a North/South link line which would eventually carry Severn Tunnel traffic north, through Ross, Hereford, Shrewsbury, Chester and on to Manchester and Liverpool, by-passing the congested Midlands, and in so doing, the operating company the Great Western Railway could, except for a short stretch of ten miles, between Hereford and Shrewsbury, use their own company metals. The section between Shrewsbury and Hereford was owned by the Shrewsbury and Hereford Railway Company and operated jointly by the London and North Western Railway Company and the Great Western Railway.

430.—WYE VALLEY.

Incorporated by 29 and 30 Vic., cap. 357 (10th August, 1866), to construct railways from the South Wales to the Coleford Monmouth Usk and Pontypool and to the South Wales and Great Western Direct. Length, 15 miles. Capital, 230,000*l.* in 20*l.* shares, and 76,600*l.* on loan. Arrangements with Great Western and South Wales and Great Western Direct.

No. of Directors—5 ; minimum, 3 ; quorum, 3 and 2. *Qualification,* 500*l.*

DIRECTORS :

Jasper Wilson Johns, Esq., Wolverton Park, Newbury, Hants.	James Murphy, Esq.
	Joseph Cary, Esq., 49, Pall Mall, S.W.
Osmond A. Wyatt, Esq., Troy House, Monmouth.	Capt. Robert O'Brien Jameson, 60, St. James's Street, Piccadilly, S.W.

Extract from Bradshaw Railway Manual of 1870.

Construction began early in May, 1874 and by the latter half of 1876 the railway was opened to the public (Wednesday, 1st November, 1876). The Contractors were Messrs. Reed Bros. of London.

It had taken two and a half years to complete just over thirteen miles of railway from the Wye Valley Junction to Wyesham, the Civil Engineering could be split roughly into two halves, the relatively easy section north of Tintern and by far the most difficult the southern portion from Tintern to the Wye Valley Junction. The line south from Wyesham to Redbrook was relatively straightforward as regards civil engineering as there were no viaducts, tunnels or vast earth works to be undertaken. The task involved cutting a shelf along the hillside and building a secure base wide enough for a single track railway; this was achieved by using large pieces of stone to form a stable base for the ballast to lay on, this stone also provided ideal hillside drainage. Large stone blocks can still be seen alongside the track bed between Wyesham and Tintern. A steadily decreasing incline is apparent as the construction work nears Redbrook. Here a bridge and viaduct had to be built, the bridge was to carry the line over the A466 road and the viaduct, a much more splendid affair to carry the railway over the River Wye to Penallt. The viaduct was built on a gentle curve and has an overall span of just over three hundred feet, it is an iron girder construction supported by four pairs of cast iron columns. Moving south again from Penallt to Brockweir the engineering involved on this part of the route was very light as the railway followed close to the river on the flat valley floor; construction work consisted solely of providing a sound track bed that was adequately drained. The drainage arches can still be seen intact between Penallt and Whitebrook. These arches were necessary to allow passage of natural springs and streams beneath the track bed. From Brockweir to Tintern the line begins to climb away from the river on an incline of 1 in 80 rising steadily to a height of 60 feet at the river bank just south of Tintern Station, where the line finished in a vertical drop in the form of a stone parapet. This embankment was needed in order to bring the track level up to the same height as that of the land on the opposite east bank of the Wye, where the railway recrossed the river via a single iron span bridge having a length of 207 feet (the centre section was removed in the late 1960's).

The bridge was supported by tubular pillars and two stone buttresses one on each bank, the larger on the east bank is built into the near vertical sides of a tongue of land that juts out into the river. It is here at Tintern that the first and the shorter of the two tunnels on the line was built. It constitutes what would be taken for the Tintern village by-pass, for it was bored through a peninsula of land that is situated directly opposite the village. The tunnel is 182 yards long and was cut through sandstone of the carboniferous type, the northern portal being situated directly beneath the monks path that led from Tintern Abbey to the Malthouse at Brockweir.

From the outset the planning, surveying and civil engineering of the southern portion, the Shorn Cliff section of track between Tintern and Tidenham, was to prove extremely difficult, this was due to the unfavourable topography, which consisted of steep gradients that drew the land towards the river as it neared the estuary. To add to this difficult terrain the steep slopes were covered with dense undergrowth, which made the construction work all the more difficult.

The plan for the Shorn Cliff section was to cut a shelf in the hillside between the two tunnels, Tintern and Tidenham, wide enough for a single track railway and then support the earthwork each side of the line with stone walls, below track level on the riverside and above on the land side, therefore preventing the danger of landslips. These walls now much overgrown still remain intact.

The engineer's plan called for a viaduct to be built along the Shorn Cliff section; this structure was named Black Morgan Viaduct, situated a quarter of a mile south of Wireworks Junction. The structure has an overall span of 140 feet and is supported by three semi-eliptical arches.

Immediately south of Black Morgan Viaduct the steep gradient of the hillside begins to ease, making construction work less difficult. It is along this section that a stone drainage arch was built with a span of fifteen feet it permits access to the river for a small stream and nowadays shelter for a local herd of cattle.

The easy gradient is only evident for a short distance, a quarter of a mile or so north of Tintern Quarry, before the geography takes a turn for the worse, as far as railway engineering is concerned, for here a massive rock face comes into sight and the entrance of the second tunnel of which the northern portal marks the place where the railway crosses the ancient fortification of Offa's Dyke.

Without doubt, the most difficult and physically enduring work on the line, took place here, with the boring of the Tidenham or Denhill Tunnel as it is sometimes referred to. Here great quantities of material had to be moved, it proved a formidable task and consumed the greater part of the budget. The boring took two years to complete and was grossly underestimated in cost and length, being one thousand one hundred and eighty-eight yards long on completion, compared with the original estimate of seven hundred and fifteen yards, making it eventually the twenty-first longest tunnel on the Great Western Railway.

The tunnel was cut through a land mass consisting mainly of limestone, which rose nearly seven hundred and fifty feet from the River

Wye below; it faces a well known landmark in the lower region of the Wye Valley called the Wynd Cliff. Messrs. Reed Bros., recorded for that time a remarkable rate of progress with the boring, their 'navvies' (from navigators i.e., builders of canals which they had been originally, in many cases) managed to bore just under six feet a day; a monumental task considering that the workmen had to shift large amounts of earth and rock the hard way by muscle, pick and shovel as mechanical aids were few and rudimentary. On completion, the boring of the tunnel had taken just under 20 months to complete.

South of Tidenham Tunnel the construction work was much easier and to prevent unnecessary gradients a shallow cutting was excavated starting at the southern portal of the tunnel and finishing just prior to Tidenham Station a distance of just under three quarters of a mile. The bridge immediately south of Tidenham station was built to carry the line over the A48, the main Chepstow to Gloucester Road, this originally wooden sided bridge has one iron span supported by two stone built parapets. The structure underwent a major overhaul in 1978 during which parts of the centre span was strengthened and the wooden sides were replaced with metal sections. The bridge also marks the start of a long, high embankment that carries the railway for three quarters of a mile gradually turning west on a steadily decreasing incline of 1 in 66 finishing at the Wye Valley Junction giving access to the South Wales/Gloucester main line and consequently Chepstow via Brunels magnificent Wye Bridge.

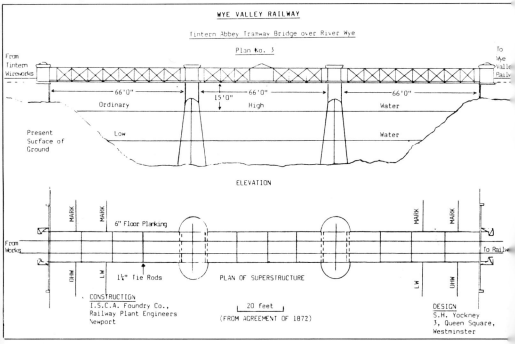

WYE VALLEY RAILWAY

Tintern Abbey Tramway Bridge over River Wye

Plan No. 3

The modified version of the Armstrong 0-4-2T, a type which worked the branch until the early thirties; this photo was taken about 1908.

Monmouth Troy Station, 24th March, 1951; taken from the B4293 road which crosses over the Pontypool line via the tunnel at the west end of the platform. Nearest the camera on the left is 0-4-2T No. 1445 pulling auto trailer No. W174 on the 9.25 a.m. to Ross-on-Wye. In front and making ready to leave is 0-6-0PT No. 6415 coupled to auto trailer W153 with the Wye Valley train on the 9.10 a.m. to Newport calling at all stations and halts in between. To the right of the picture is rail car No. 30 awaiting departure with the 9.10 a.m. to Pontypool Road. (W. A. Camwell).

Monmouth Troy looking east, in June 1922. (R. S. Carpenter).

The 7.45 p.m. Monmouth Troy to Severn Tunnel Junction with 0-6-0 PT No. 6426 at Netherhope Halt. (B. L. Jenkins).

Brockweir Halt, 15th October, 1958; approaching the Halt is 0-6-0 Pannier Tank No. 6426 on the 11.50 a.m. Monmouth Troy—Chepstow and Newport train. The River Wye was in flood, highlighting the close proximity of the river and railway at this point. (W. A. Camwell).

St. Briavels station, built in 1876, underwent several name changes from its original title Bigsweir. The first alteration came in May, 1909 when it was renamed St. Briavels and Llandogo. Llandogo was dropped on 1st February, 1927 in anticipation of the opening of Llandogo Halt. The complex consisted of the station buildings, goods shed, signal box, level crossing and storage shed. The signal box was closed in November, 1928 and control of the loop and sidings was given over to ground frame levers. The station was closed to passenger and freight in January, 1959. The station and goods shed still remains on the site along with remnants of the level crossing gates and the only moveable distant signal on the entire line. (B. M. Handley).

Redbrook-on-Wye station consisted of a station building, goods shed and signal box, which controlled the loop and sidings that were situated at the southern end of the platform. By October, 1925 the signal box was manned only when required and was closed altogether in January, 1927 control of the sidings being given over to ground frame levers. The entire site was demolished in the late sixties and the restaurant now stands near to the site of the old station. A G.W.R. boundary post still in situ marks the southern border of the Redbrook sidings. (W. A. Camwell).

Railcar No. RC30 at Tintern on 21st June, 1951, working the 2.40 p.m. from Chepstow to Monmouth. (W. A. Camwell).

Tintern Railway Bridge (Wireworks Branch): The upkeep of this structure was the sole responsibility of the Wye Valley Railway Company. The bridge became a prominent nail in the Company's coffin. Three spans 60 ft. at 38 ft. high (drawing Gwent County Records Office P & BR 421). (B. M. Handley).

Monmouth Troy Station, March 1951. The train with 0-6-0PT No. 6415 waiting to leave is the 9.10 a.m. Wye Valley train to Newport stopping at all halt and stations in between; auto-trailer No. W153. Of note are the covered footbridge and the refreshment room, unusual additions to find on a country branch station. On the right-hand side of the photograph can be seen a tunnel entrance; it is all that remains of the Monnow valley project of 1865. This was a scheme to construct a line from Monmouth to Pontrilas; unfortunately the contractor, Thomas Savin, went bankrupt and the scheme failed. (W. A. Camwell).

D37210 'Running around' at Tintern Quarry in July, 1979. Between Wireworks Junction and Tidenham Tunnel is situated Tintern Quarry which belongs to W. G. Turrif Ltd. The siding connection to the Quarry was brought into use in February, 1931 and consisted of one ground frame to the north of the quarry and a stretch of track leading to the hopper loading bay. This siding remained in situ until April, 1964 when an additional ground frame was laid giving a southern access to the sidings. From August, 1964 the Wye Valley Junction to Tintern Quarry has been worked as a private siding. (B. M. Handley).

Penallt Halt was opened on the 1st August, 1971. Situated as it was on the west bank of the Wye, only the Viaduct, the entrance of which is next to the telegraph pole separated it from Redbrook, making them some of the closest stopping places on the whole Railway network. (Lens of Sutton).

The last passenger train from Tintern; ex-G.W.R. 0-6-0PT No. 6412 propelled the train to Monmouth with No. 6439 pulling, and the train reversed at Monmouth for Ross-on-Wye; 4th January, 1959. (B. L. Jenkins).

No. D37238 emerging from the heavily overgrown southern portal of Tidenham tunnel with a Down ballast train. Netherhope Halt was situated on the right of the photograph. (B. M. Handley).

A down freight for Chepstow passing the Wye Valley Junction in June, 1979, the beginning and end of the Wye Valley Branch. This is also the site of the old terminal station known as Chepstow East, which existed until the early 1850's. Its closure was due to the opening of Brunel's Bridge over the River Wye which did away with the need for terminal stations each side of the river. The Junction was once controlled by the Wye Valley Junction signal box which was situated on the right of the picture where the heap of rubble now lies. The box was closed in March, 1969 and the branch is now under the supervision of the Chepstow signal box. (B. M. Handley).

Trespass notice, left (G. Mead) and Boundary Post (B. M. Handley)

It was stated on the original prospectus of 1874 that the line from Monmouth to Tintern was to be completed by the 25th March of that year and the rest by the 31st December, 1875. Immediately upon completion, the line was to be taken over by the Great Western Railway as the operating company. In reality the completion date was exceeded by several months with the line being finally completed by the Autumn of 1876.

The opening day was a grand affair in true victorian style, in attendance were the Directors and Engineers of the W.V.R. Company and the officials of the G.W.R. The special train left Chepstow just after mid-day on the 28th October, 1876. The first stop was Tintern, where an invitation to visit the Abbey had been extended by His Grace the Duke of Beaufort, lunch was later served in the grounds of the Beaufort Arms, Tintern.

The party was then taken on to Monmouth where a cordial reception was awaiting them. Bells were ringing and the whole town had turned out to see the special train arrive. The corporation led by the Mayor were assembled on Monmouth Troy Station, waiting to greet the visitors and conduct them through the town and the crowds of cheering people, to the Beaufort Arms Hotel, where speeches were made and toasts were drank, to celebrate the occasion. For the party's return journey, Tintern Abbey, Tidenham Tunnel and the cliffs along the valley were lit with changing coloured lights. Unfortunately this happy note on which the railway began was not to continue. For twenty nine years the Wye Valley Railway Company battled for its existence.

The railway was worked and leased in perpetuity by the Great Western Railway, upon the terms of the G.W.R. Co. paying the W.V.R. Co. for the first five years a rent of 55% of gross receipts. And after that period of 50% of gross receipts. One important advantage which accrued to the W.V.R. Co. from the agreement with the G.W.R. was that its revenue would not be affected in any way by the cost of working expenses, as the W.V.R. Co. would be entitled under all circumstances to receive the above mentioned fixed proportion of the gross receipts, totally independent of what may be the cost of working the line. This agreement would seem to have been ideal to the W.V.R. But as the following extracts taken from reports of Shareholders' Meetings dated 1876—1904 show, the company repeatedly made financial losses and continued on a shoe string existence. The losses were credited to various factors, for example, bad weather, which had a detrimental effect on the much valued tourist trade, the running down and eventual closure of many of the manufacturing industries of the lower Wye Valley, and to a lesser extent, the continuous squabbles and disagreements that were a prominent feature between the owning company and the operating company, which inevitably led to poor services and lack of maintenance, turning the much needed public support against the railway. Lastly and undoubtedly the greatest cross the W.V.R. Co. had to bear was the unprofitable Tintern Railway or Wireworks Branch.

All these factors proved too great for the W.V.R. Board of Directors, which itself had experienced problems, arising from mismanagement of company affairs and certain irregularities with company funds. In March, 1881 these irregularities led to legal action being taken against the Chairman, Mr. W. Hawes and other members of the board, yet another blow to the ill-fated railway.

The Wye Valley Railway's five working years from 1876—1881 under Hawes's control had gone from bad to worse and culminated in the Shareholders appointing a receiver, a Mr. Edwin Waterhouse, to sort out the companies' ailing affairs. The first move was to appoint a new Chairman and Board of Directors. The new appointments were made, a Mr. A. Jerrard (Chairman), Mr. F. W. Raikes, Mr. E. Toovey and Mr. B. Joyner. This time it was also decided on the inclusion of a fifth board member. The Rev. William Dyke was invited to join the board and he accepted the appointment. Perhaps the idea of a man of God overseeing the affairs of the railway would prevent a reoccurrence of past events.

The new board set about their task with fervour but unfortunately the railway was unable to recover and build itself a firm financial base. The W.V.R. company finally collapsed towards the closing months of 1889 and for the second time in its short erratic history a receiver was again appointed, this time to wind up the railway's affairs and to handle the eventual amalgamation with the Great Western Railway.

Proposals for the sale of the railway were first started with the G.W.R. in the closing months of 1887. Terms for the amalgamation were agreed upon by both companies and everything would have gone ahead smoothly, but for the intervention of Mr. Read, a newly appointed director to the W.V.R. board. He stopped the proceedings by sending letters to the shareholders telling them to buy their own shares and not to agree to the sale of the railway. This last initiative was short lived as the remaining directors resigned a few months later.

In December, 1904 Wye Valley Railway shareholders received a circular from their Chairman J. H. Whatcoat informing them yet again, of the deteriorating state of the company. The letter went on to explain the negotiations, that were taking place with the Great Western Railway. In monetary terms the Great Western Railway Company was offering £12.10s.0d. for each £100 preference stock and 10s. for each £20 ordinary share. The G.W.R. offer was unanimously acepted by the Wye Valley Shareholders.

The following summarised extracts from directors' annual reports to shareholders from 1877—1904 tell some of the story:

MARCH 28th, 1879: The receipts continue to improve. Passengers carried in last six months have been 54,234 against 38,555 in the six months ending June, 30th, 1878. An increase of 40% and the goods 14,640 tons against 11,373 an increase of 28%. The gross receipts for the half year have been £2,836.14s.1d. against £2,098.19s.4d. for the half year ending June 30th, 1878 an increase of 35%.

11th SEPTEMBER, 1879: Receipts down to £1,975.4s.11d. Most unsatisfactory. But due to wetness of season and depression of trade.

MARCH, 1881: Wireworks Branch constructed at needless expense. Thought by directors a source of considerable gain as much traffic uses line. However, company have no power to receive tolls in respect of branch. So have no funds for its maintenance but trust that G.W.R. will see advantage to them of keeping it open.

SEPTEMBER, 1881: Lost money again (£53.18s.1d.) caused by diversion of traffic from Bristol over Severn Bridge after pier at Portskewett had been burned. Company offered wharves but G.W.R. declined (prejudicial to company).

MARCH, 1882: Receipts still falling. Causing anxiety but not without hope. G.W.R. still being awkward—refusing facilities for passenger traffic etc.,

DECEMBER, 1882: Increase of over £500: would have been more but Redbrook tinplate works closed G.W.R. being more liberal—residents of locality sent petition to G.W.R. for improved services.

DECEMBER, 1883: Still losing money, negotiations with Golden Valley Railway Company for running powers over line, but G.V. Co., not yet applied for Parliamentary powers.

DECEMBER, 1904: Letters sent to shareholders stating terms of G.W.R. Each £100 Wye Valley Railway 5% debenture stock to be exchanged for equal amounts of G.W.R. 4½% stock. £12.10s.0d. in cash to be given for each £100 of W.V.R. preference stock. 10s. per share for each W.V.R. ordinary share. Payment of £600 to discharge liabilities. W.V.R. now indebted to G.W.R. about £30,000.

Total amalgamation with the G.W.R. was completed by 1st July, 1905, and as far as the travelling public were concerned the relinquishing of power by the W.V.R. was a good thing; as now the railway came under total control of the G.W.R., improved services were soon evident and maintenance that had fallen behind was rectified. The service became fairly consistent throughout the year with four or five trains a day in each direction, operating on a Monday to Saturday timetable. This service was complemented by additional trains introduced after 1918. This was a Summer Sunday service to take advantage of the weekend tourists to this world famous beauty spot. The excursions were operated consistently up to the early part of 1939 when they were finally dropped due to the outbreak of war.

While under G.W.R. control other alterations gradually took place to improve the service to the local community, new halts were opened to complement the four rather widespread orginal stations. The halts added in chronological order were Whitebrook, Llandogo, Brockweir, Wyesham, Penallt and finally Netherhope. Special instructions were issued for the working of trains along the branch. The following is an extract from a special instruction manual issued to Station Masters and Guards and dated June, 1889.

Wye Valley Railway

Trains not exceeding seven vehicles—Rear vehicles to be braked, a guard to ride in it.

Trains comprising eight to fourteen vehicles — Front and rear vehicles to be brakes, a guard to ride in each.

Trains comprising fifteen to twenty vehicles — Front and rear vehicles and vehicle in centre of train to be brakes and a guard to ride in each.

The greatest movement of traffic on the branch took place during the Summer months which made the signalman's job a busy one, owing to the fact that the branch was single line throughout its entire length, with the exception of a few passing loops. From the Wye Valley Junction to Wyesham the line was divided into six sections.

Like many rural services across the country, the Wye Valley Line suffered gradual losses in revenue during the inter war period (1918-1939) there were several reasons for this decline in the railway popularity. The most immediate and obvious being the gradual improvement that was taking place in the roads and the steady rise in the use of motor transport. The internal combustion engine began to pressure the railways at a local and national level on three fronts i.e. lorries (goods traffic) buses (passenger transport) and to a much lesser extent motor cars (private traffic). There were efforts made by the G.W.R. to attract people back to the line by introducing steam trailers and at a later date the rail car, a simple and cheap mode of carrying light passenger traffic. But unfortunately the writing was on the wall; even before the publication of the Beeching Report, the line was realised to be uneconomical. It was costing British Railways in excess of £20,000 per annum when the decision was taken to abandon passenger traffic, and it had become obvious that the area was better served by the more efficient road transport. The line was officially closed to passenger traffic on Monday, 5th January, 1959. Goods traffic continued to operate for five more years and was finally withdrawn in January, 1964.

The last passenger train to use the branch was an eight-coach special train, probably the longest on the line since the hey day of the Tintern excursions and composed entirely of ex-G.W.R. stock, it left Chepstow at 11.20 a.m., motive power being ex-G.W.R. 0-6-0 pannier tanks No. 6439 pulling and No. 6412 propelling, until the train's first reversal at Monmouth. Railway pensioners and others connected with the line travelled on the train, augmenting the numbers to some four hundred and eight, including a Mr. Palmer, farmer at St. Briavels, whose father and grandmother travelled on the first train of the Wye Valley Railway, and whose grandfather became a farmer of substance by supplying the local contractors engaged in the extended excavation of Tidenham Tunnel, the longest on the line.

After a fine view of the snow encircled ruins of Tintern Abbey and a glimpse on emerging from Tintern Tunnel of a trespass warning board bearing the name 'Wye Valley Railway', the train halted briefly at Tintern Station. After passing St. Briavels and its crossing box with the only moveable distants on the whole line, the next stop was Redbrook-on-Wye separated from the preceding Penallt Halt only by the viaduct over the River Wye.

With a view of the site of the abandoned Coleford Branch descending steeply from the woods to the east the aproach to Monmouth Troy was heralded uniquely, even for a last train, by a pelting with snowballs as it passed the housing estate on the outskirts of Monmouth adjoining Wyesham Halt.

Perhaps this unusual sight for a Monmouthshire Sunday could not be endured by local inhabitants, for very few, considering the size of the town, witnessed the final closure to passenger traffic of the last two of Monmouth's one-time four branches.

For nearly ninety years steam locomotives had wound their sinuous course up and down the Wye Valley. Being pulled along in a smartly painted carriage was a leisurely experience evocative of an age when 'time' was considered less important than it is today. On a Summer afternoon with the fresh country air blowing through the carriage windows the fourteen and a half mile journey from Monmouth to

Chepstow would take forty five to fifty minutes with the train stopping at eight halts and four stations. For the tourist the branch provided superb views of the Wye Valley and its magnificent surrounding countryside.

Had Monmouth remained the County town of Monmouthshire (Gwent) it would have been the first County town to ever have lost its passenger service.

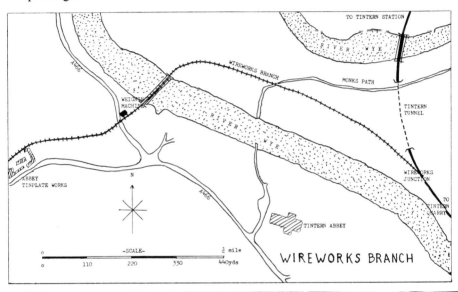

CHEPSTOW, MONMOUTH, and COLEFORD (1st and 3rd class).—Great Western.

Miles.	Up.	Week Days.					Miles.	Down.	Week Days.					NOTES.
		mrn	mrn	mrn	mrn	aft			mrn	mrn	aft	aft		
	Paddington Station,							Coleford.........dep.	8 24	1135	2 15	5 26	....	
58	London ......dep.	1 b0	....	5 40	11 0	2 30	2¼	Newland.............	8 31	1142	2 28	5 35	....	
58	Bristol † .... "	5 55	....	9 45	11 15	5 30	6	Monmouth { arr.	8 45	1156	2 45	5 47	....	
—	Severn Tunnel Jn.dep.	6 50	....	1112	2 30	6 18		(Troy) 98 { dep.	8 55	1217	4 0	5 57	....	
7¼	Chepstow .... "	7 9	....	1130	2 48	6 38	8¼	Redbrook	9 3	1223	4 6	6 3	....	
9	Tidenham	7 15	....	1136	2 54	6 44	12	St. Briavels & Llandogo	9 11	1231	4 14	6 11	....	b Except Mondays
12¾	Tintern	7 25	....	1146	3 4	6 54	15¼	Tintern	9 19	1237	4 23	6 21	....	
16	St. Briavels & Llandogo	7 32	....	1153	3 11	7 1	19	Tidenham	9 27	1246	4 31	6 29	....	k Stapleton Road
19¾	Redbrook	7 39	....	12 0	3 18	7 8	20¾	Chepstow 62.....arr.	9 34	1252	4 39	6 36	....	
22	Monmouth { arr.	7 46	....	12 7	3 25	7 15	28	Severn Tunnel Jn. 58	9 52	1 29	4 57	6 52	....	† Temple Meads.
	(Troy) 98 { dep.	7 58	9 40	1255	4 45	....	44¼	62 Bristol † .... "	11 3	2 40	6 5	7 45	....	
25½	Newland	8 12	9 54	1 15	5 5	....	151½	62 London (Pad.) b	1240	6 0	1010	1145	....	
28	Coleford 606 ....arr.	8 19	10 1	1 25	5 15	....								

Passenger timetable for October 1911.

SEVERN TUNNEL, CHEPSTOW, and MONMOUTH.—Great Western.

Miles.	Up.	Week Days only.					Miles.	Down.	Week Days only.				
		mrn	mrn	aft	aft	aft			mrn	aft	aft	aft	aft
—	Severn Tunnel Jn. dep	7 42	....	1040	....	3 0	4 57	10	Monmouth (Troy)..dep.	9 5	....	12 5	....	4 05 55	....
2¼	Portskewett	7 48	....	1047	....	3 5	4 57 16	2¼	Redbrook	9 12	....	121	....	4 7 6 2	....
7¼	Chepstow { arr.	7 56	....	1055	....	3 145	0 7 24	6	St. Briavels & Llandogo	9 21	....	124	....	4 166 11	....
	{ dep.	7 58	....	1058	....	3 165	17 25	9¼	Tintern, for Brockweir	9 29	....	129	....	4 246 19 0	....
9	Tidenham	8 ..	....	11 5	....	3 235	87 33	13	Tidenham	9 40	....	1240	....	4 356 39 8 10	....
12¾	Tintern, for Brockweir	8 17	....	1117	....	3 345	197 43	14	Chepstow 71 { arr.	9 46	....	1246	....	4 416 36 8 16	....
16	St. Briavels & Llandogo	8 24	....	1124	....	3 415	26		{ dep.	9 42	....	1250	....	4 426 38 8 18	....
19¾	Redbrook	8 32	....	1138	....	3 505	35	19¾	Portskewett ...... {60, 659 55	....	1259	....	4 506 46	....
22	Monmouth (Troy) 72 arr.	8 41	....	1142	....	3 585	43	22	Severn Tunnel Jn. arr.	10 0	....	1 4	....	4 566 518 30	....

☞ For OTHER TRAINS between Severn Tunnel Junction and Chepstow, see page 71.

Passenger timetable for July 1922.

As already mentioned the Wye Valley Railway was constructed primarily as a north/south link; the alignment of the track was of paramount importance as the fastest route between Wyesham and the Wye Valley Junction was obviously the most direct.

The route finally agreed upon was laid for the greater part on the east bank of the river and effectively by-passed Tintern by going via the second shorter 'Tintern Tunnel'. The tunnel was cut through a promontory of land that projects westward and is situated across the river from Tintern village. The line emerges from the tunnel for one hundred yards or so before eventually crossing the river just south of the village, this meant that Tintern Station was situated some way out of the village much to the dissatisfaction of the locals and Messrs. Murrell and Stothart, lessees of the Tintern Abbey Wireworks. But nevertheless it was a sound economical move on behalf of the W.V.R. as the site served not only Tintern but Brockweir as well. (Brockweir was to gain its own halt on the 23rd September, 1929).

With the growing concern over the alignment of the railway, representations were eventually made to the Duke of Beaufort being the owner of the land, by the lessees of the Wireworks and the people of Tintern to lodge their disappointment at being by-passed by the railway. This action culminated in a formal agreement being signed on 22nd November, 1872 between the Wye Valley Railway Company on the one hand and the Duke of Beaufort and his son the Marquess of Worcester on the other, in which the company undertook to build a branch railway across the river to serve the Tintern Abbey Wireworks only. The locals still had to use the official station.

The Wye Valley Amendment Act was passed on the 14th June, 1875 (W.V.R. Amendment Act. 38 Vict. CAP. LL). The Act contained the following provision amongst others:

The line was to be reserved for the exclusive use of the landowners and their tenants.

It was to be completed by the 1st November, 1874 or with the main line if that was completed before.

The Company was to 'forever maintain the branch and junction in repair'.

No charge was to be made for goods to or from the Wireworks, in respect of the branch by the company.

All vehicles were to be supplied by the company for the transport of goods to and from the Wireworks.

A bridge was to be constructed, capable of bearing a locomotive and three loaded trucks at least, and was to have a clear headway of 15′ above the ordinary high water mark.

The engineers and contractors for the project were the same as for the main line. Work commenced in June, 1874 and the engineers reported in August 1875 that the line was complete and ready for use. Unfortunately by this time Messrs. Murrell and Stothart had gone out of business. The branch lay dormant until the early 1880's when the works were taken over by Josiah Richards, John Rowland Griffiths and David Williams, collectively known as the Tintern Abbey Wire and Tinplate Company. This new venture was short lived and by 1901 trading had ceased altogether. It was also the end of steam traction on the branch as the privately owned locomotive was sold in February 1902 during the dismantling of the works. However, traffic did not cease on the branch completely as Messrs. J. Jones and Son who owned the sawmills and turnery works in Tintern used horse-powered traction to convey goods between their premises and Wireworks Junction. Traffic continued in this fashion until the mid 1930's when the track had deteriorated to such an extent that reconstruction would have been too costly an exercise.

It will be noticed that the W.V.R. were responsible for supplying the rolling stock used on the branch. In reality the rolling stock was supplied by the G.W.R. as the operating company. There is no mention in the Agreement of any locomotive supplied in fact throughout the branch lines precarious existence a sign appeared near the junction with the main line forbidding G.W.R. locomotives to enter the branch, with an exception of ten yards or so that led to a gate which closed the branch when not in use. This sign was in fact contadictory to a statement made by S. H. Yockney to the press at the opening ceremony, when he inferred that the Wireworks Branch would enable railway access to Tintern village and the Abbey ruins for the travelling public. The motive power for the branch line was supplied and maintained by the Tintern Abbey Works. It would seem to have taken the form of an 0-4-0 vertical boilered locomotive having a large covered cab and two vertical outside cylinders. It was known locally as 'The coffee pot'. The engine was capable of hauling six loaded wagons at one time and with the absence of a 'run round' facility at the junction the push pull method was in use.

From the opening day the Tintern Railway or Wireworks Branch was to prove a veritable millstone around the W.V.R. company's neck, as no tolls or charges could be made for its use and the operating company, the G.W.R., refused to take any responsibility for the upkeep and repair. The branch itself was finally made useless by the intense heat of the Summer of 1935 which buckled the rails, they were subsequently lifted and sold in 1941. The junction with the main line was the last part to be removed in January, 1945.

From the opening of the Wye Valley line the G.W.R. were responsible for the motive power and rolling stock and being a branch line the locomotives were generally of the 517 light tank class introduced by Joseph Armstrong (C.M.E. of the G.W.R. 1864—1877). These excellent locomotives built at Wolverhampton from 1868—1885 were the 0-4-2 branch line tank engines recognisable by their burnished brass domes, round eyed windows and jaunty shaped copper capped chimneys. Some years later in 1895 there were several more slightly modified additions to the class, their innovations included outside bearings for the trailing wheels; the boiler pressures varied from 150—165 lbs developing a tractive effort between 12,635 lbs to a maximum of 14,780 lbs. Two types of cylinder sizes were used, 16" x 24" and 16½" x 24"; the valve gear was of the Stephenson type. The first locomotive was withdrawn from service in 1904, but the class continued to operate until 1945 when the last locomotive was withdrawn.

These attractive little tanks remained with the Wye Valley Branch virtually unchanged until the early 1930's when under the direction of Charles B. Collett most of the early Victorian branch line locomotives were replaced by modified and improved designs of which the 14XX and 64XX tank classes were examples. These new locomotives were larger and more powerful and being fitted with larger coal bunkers than the 517 class were capable of longer terms of duty before having to refuel. The majority of the new locomotives were fitted with push and pull apparatus which made them ideal for single line working.

Between 1932 and 1936 almost one hundred of the new 14XX class tanks were turned out at Swindon: they weighed just over forty one tons and had 5' 2" driving wheels with 16" x 24" cylinders. The boiler had a working pressure of 165 P.S.I. delivering a tractive effort of 13,900 lbs. These locomotives having a tractive effort below 16,500 lbs were ungrouped and were more or less unrestricted in their route capabilities. Newport, Ebbw. Pontypool Road and Hereford were the sheds that served the Wye Valley Branch, and they were assigned several of the new 14XX class tanks of which numbers 1421, 1445, 1455, were to stay with the Wye Valley Branch until its closure, sharing daily duties with pannier tanks mainly of the 0-6-0 64XX class also built at Swindon during the same period. These were heavier locomotives than the 14XX class weighing 45 tons 12 cwt., but their driving wheels were slightly smaller at 4' 7½". They were fitted with 16½" x 24" cylinders and produced a boiler pressure of 180 lbs P.S.I. This gave the locomotives a working tractive effort of 18,010 lbs qualifying the class for power Class A and a yellow route restriction colour. Numbers 6412, 6415, 6426, 6430, 6439 were examples of the class that were assigned duties along the branch.

25

The saddest duty in the history of the branch was given to two pannier tanks of this class, numbers 6412 and 6439. They pulled the last passenger train to make the journey between Monmouth and Chepstow. The latter of the two locomotives was lucky enough to escape the fate of the breakers' yard when it was withdrawn from service in November, 1964, and purchased for preservation by the Dart Valley Railway where it stayed until 1972 when it was subsequently transferred to the Torbay Steam Railway to operate along the former seven mile G.W.R. line between Paignton and Kingsweir.

The 14XX and 64XX classes were occasionally supplemented by 57XX class tanks and a fireman who worked on the branch in the late thirties told me he could remember cooking breakfast on his shovel in the sidings at Tintern, at various times over the fires of two 57XX class tanks numbers 5714 and 9745.

During the 1930's the Wye Valley like so many other branch lines up and down the country saw the introduction of the Auto trailer. This was a passenger vehicle that had a special compartment at one end fitted out with a steam regulator, brake and other controls so that when the unit was connected to the locomotive the train could be driven as normally from the footplate of the engine or alternatively from the separate driving compartment in the passenger vehicle where the driving controls had been duplicated. These new auto trains provided a basic economy in time and fuel as the locomotive did not have to uncouple and 'run round' at each terminus. The units themselves were 60′ 0″ long and 9′ 0″ wide and had a carrying capacity of 56 passengers. All major railways made some use of these push pull auto trains or auto cars, the G.W.R. having the most, employing them on many of its picturesque country routes. W153W, W174W and W237W were regularly scheduled turns of duty along the Wye Valley line towards the end of the 1950's.

Steam did not altogether have the exclusive rights of providing tractive power for the Wye Valley line, from the 1940's onwards the diesel engine began to make an appearance on many little used routes such as the country branches taking over mainly passenger duties. This new mode of rail transport took the form of the diesel railcar, and No. 30 was first assigned to the Wye Valley Branch during the early part of 1941. Railcar construction was authorised in February, 1938 and No. 30 was one of a complement of twenty built shortly after that date. The bodies and undercarriages were built at Swindon; the body had an overall length of 62′ 0″ and a maximum width of 9′ 0″, the tare weight being 35 tons 13 cwts. The motors were supplied by the Automotive Engineering Company and consisted of two direct injection, 105 horse power units of a 120 millimetre bore and 142 millimetre stroke. The bogey units had a wheel base of 8′ 6″ and the centres were 43′ 6″ apart. The wheels had a 3′ 2″ diameter. The cars were fitted with standard draw gear and mechanical transmission and geared down to give a maximum speed of 40 m.p.h. in order to provide sufficient tractive effort for hauling a tail load of up to 60 tons. The seating arrangement had a centre gangway with groups of four seats either side, making a total passenger seating capacity of 48 persons.

Locomotive Types and Examples of Classes used on the Wye Valley Railway

0-4-2T *Armstrong 517 Class*

156 Built between	... ...	1868—1885
Weight	... ...	35—40 tons
Boiler Pressure	... ...	150—165 lbs.
Cylinders	... ...	16" × 24"—16½" × 24"
Tractive Effort	... ...	12,635 lbs.—14,780 lbs.
Valve gear	... ...	Stephenson Type
Wheel diameter	... ...	5' 2"

Examples on W.V. railway: No. 217; 1466 (1466 preserved at Didcot by the G.W.R. Society).

0-6-0 *ST/PT Dean 1076: Buffalo double framed*

266 built between	... ...	1870—1881
Weight	... ...	39—45 tons
Boiler Pressure	... ...	165 lbs.
Cylinders	... ...	16" × 24"
Tractive Effort	... ...	17,525 lbs.
Valve gear	... ...	Stephenson Type
Wheel diameter	... ...	4' 7½"

Examples on W.V. railway: Nos. 754, 1180, 1254, 1637.
On 7 March, 1925, No. 1254 was derailed near Whitebrook.

G.W.R. Railcars

20 built.		
Weight	... ...	35 tons 13 cwts.
Overall length	... ...	62' 0"
Overall width	... ...	9' 0"
Motors × 2	... ...	105 h.p. each.

Examples on W.V. railway: Nos. W21W, W30W.

0-4-2T *Collett 14XX Class*

98 built between	... ...	1932—1936
Weight	... ...	41 tons
Boiler Pressure	... ...	165 lbs.
Cylinders	... ...	16" x 24"
Tractive Effort	... ...	13,900 lbs.
Valve gear	... ...	Stephenson Type
Wheel diameter	... ...	5' 2"

Examples on W.V. railway: Nos. 1401, 1404, 1421, 1445, 1455.
No. 1421 was transferred to the Culme Valley Branch on closure.

0-6-0 PT Collett 75XX Class

Built between	...	...	1929—1948
Weight	...	...	49 tons
Boiler Pressure	...	...	200 lbs./sq. in.
Cylinders	...	...	17½″ × 24″
Tractive Effort	...	...	22,515 lbs.
Valve gear	...	...	Stephenson Type
Wheel diameter	...	...	4′ 7½″

Examples on W.V. railway: Nos. 3726, 3728, 4671, 5714, 5729, 7712, 7764, 7774, 9619, 9711, 9745.

0-6-0 T Collett 64XX Class

Built between	...	...	1932—1936
Weight	...	...	45 tons
Boiler Pressure	...	...	180 lbs.
Cylinders	...	...	16½″ × 24″
Tractive Effort	...	...	18,010 lbs.
Valve gear	...	...	Stephenson Type
Wheel diameter	...	...	4′ 7½″

Examples on W.V. railway: Nos. 6400, 6403, 6412, 6415, 6417, 6424, 6426, 6429, 6430, 6439. (6412 preserved by the West Somerset Railway; 6439 preserved by the Dart Valley Railway).

CROSSING ARRANGEMENTS

Wyesham Junction and Tintern are the only intermediate Crossing Stations.

No. 4 up passenger to pass No. 3 up goods at Tintern.

No. 3 up goods to cross Nos. 4 and 5 down passenger trains at Wyesham Junction.

No. 6 down goods to cross No. 7 up passenger at Tintern.

No. 9 down passenger train will cross No. 9 up passenger train at Tintern.

The 10.25 a.m. Goods Chepstow to Monmouth will work a trip from Tintern to the Wire Works Siding with traffic when absolutely necessary.

The single line between Monmouth (Troy) and Wye Valley Junction is worked by Train Staff and Auxiliary Block Telegraph.

Three Train Staff are in use as follows:

Between Wye Valley Junction and Tintern: form of staff and tickets round—colour white.

Between Tintern and Wyesham Junction: form of staff and tickets, square—colour yellow.

Between Monmouth (Troy) and Wyesham Junction: form of staff and tickets, triangular—colour green.

SPECIAL NOTICES: All down trains proceeding towards Chepstow must stop dead at Tidenham for 'Line Clear'. Goods trains must also stop at the south end of Tidenham Tunnel, when required, to pin down brakes. Goods trains proceeding to Monmouth must stop at Wyesham Junction when required, to pin down brakes.

DOWN TRAINS.

Distance from Monmouth (Troy) Mls.	Chs.	STATIONS.	1 Coleford Passenger arr.	dep.	2 Passenger arr.	dep.	3 Coleford Passenger arr.	dep.	4 Passenger arr.	dep.	Coleford Mixed Train arr.	dep.
0	—	Monmouth (Troy)	A.M. —	A.M. 8 7	A.M. —	A.M. 8 50	A.M. —	A.M. 9 20	P.M. —	P.M. 12 35	P.M. —	P.M. 12 50
0	61	Wyesham Junc.	8	8 10	9 13	9 16	9	…	12 38	12 42	12	12 55
2	22	Redbrook	…	…	9 22	9 33	…	…	12 49	12 50	…	…
5	62	Bigswear	…	…	9 30	9 31	…	…	12 58	1 0	…	…
9	12	Tintern	…	…	9 30	9 31	…	…	1 —	1 11	…	…
9	45	Wire Works Junc.	…	…	…	…	…	…	…	…	…	…
12	77	Tidenham	…	…	9 39	9 41	…	…	1 17	—	…	…
13	67	Wye Valley Junc.	…	…	9 47	9 50	…	…	1 14	1 20	…	…
14	44	Chepstow	…	…	9 58	—	…	…	1 30	—	…	…
19	8	Portskewett	…	…	…	…	…	…	1 30	—	…	…

STATIONS.	6 Goods arr.	dep.	7 Passenger arr.	dep.	8 Coleford Mix. Train arr.	dep.	9 Passenger arr.	dep.
Monmouth (Troy)	P.M. —	P.M. 1 15	P.M. —	P.M. 4 0	P.M. —	P.M. 4 45	P.M. —	P.M. 6 10
Wyesham Junc.	1 30	1 45	4 6	4 3	50	…	6 16	6 13
Redbrook	2 0	2 15	—	4 7	…	…	6 24	6 17
Bigswear	2 20 X	2 30	4 14	4 25	…	…	6 33	6 25
Tintern	CR	…	4 23	4 25	…	…	6 44	6 35
Wire Works Junc.	…	…	…	…	…	…	…	…
Tidenham	3 35	3 45	4 34	4 36	…	…	6 52	6 46
Wye Valley Junc.	—	30	4 42	39	…	…	—	6 55
Chepstow	3 55	—	4 53	—	…	…	7 5	—
Portskewett	▲		4 45	—	5 55	—		

▲ This Train will be banked to Wyesham Junction when necessary, but the load must not exceed 35 Wagons.

Up Trains.

Distance from Portskewett Mls.	Chs.	STATIONS.	1 Passenger arr.	dep.	2 Coleford Passenger arr.	dep.	3 Goods arr.	dep.	4 Passenger arr.	dep.	5 Coleford Passenger arr.	dep.
0	—	Portskewett	A.M. —	A.M. 7 5	A.M. —	A.M. …	A.M. —	A.M. 10 15	A.M. —	A.M. 10 55	P.M. —	P.M. …
4	44	Chepstow	7 15	7 17	…	…	10 22	10 30	11 5	11 7	…	…
5	21	Wye Valley Junc.	—	—	…	…	19	…	—	—	…	…
6	11	Tidenham	7 22	7 23	…	…	10 50	11 33	11 12	11 13	…	…
9	43	Wire Works Junc.	…	…	…	…	…	…	…	…	…	…
9	76	Tintern	7 33	7 35	…	…	11 45	11 50	11 23	11 25	…	…
13	26	Bigswear	7 43	7 44	…	…	12 5	12 25	11 33	11 34	…	…
16	66	Redbrook	7 52	7 54	…	…	12 30 X	12 55	11 42	11 44	…	…
18	27	Wyesham Junc.	8	57	8	57	1 0	—	11 47	—	…	…
19	8	Monmouth (Troy)	8 0	—	9 0	—	—	—	11 50	—	12 10	12 7

STATIONS.	6 Coleford Mix. Train arr.	dep.	7 Passenger arr.	dep.	8 Coleford Passenger arr.	dep.	9 Passenger arr.	dep.
Portskewett	P.M. —	P.M. …	P.M. —	P.M. 2 20	P.M. —	P.M. …	P.M. —	P.M. 5 25
Chepstow	…	…	2 30	2 33	…	…	—	5 31
Wye Valley Junc.	…	…	38	…	…	…	5	…
Tidenham	…	…	2 40	2 41	…	…	5 30	—
Wire Works Junc.	…	…	…	…	…	…	…	…
Tintern	…	…	2 51 X	2 53	…	…	5 41	5 43
Bigswear	…	…	3 1	3 12	…	…	5 51	5 52
Redbrook	…	…	3 10	3 12	…	…	6 0	6 2
Wyesham Junc.	2	40	—	15	…	52	6	5
Monmouth (Troy)	2 45	—	3 18	—	5 55	—	6 8	—

The Single Line between Monmouth (Troy) and Wye Valley Junction, is worked by Train Staff and Auxiliary Block Telegraph.

Three Train Staffs are in use as under:—

BETWEEN WYE VALLEY JUNCTION AND TINTERN.
Form of Staff and Tickets round—colour white.

BETWEEN TINTERN AND WYESHAM JUNCTION.
Form of Staff and Tickets square—colour yellow.

BETWEEN MONMOUTH (TROY) AND WYESHAM JUNCTION.
Form of Staff and Tickets triangular—colour green.

SPECIAL NOTICES.—All Down Trains proceeding towards Chepstow must stop dead at Tidenham for "Line Clear."

Goods Trains must also stop at the south end of Tidenham Tunnel, when required, to pin down Breaks. Goods Trains proceeding to Monmouth must stop at Wyesham Junction, when required, to pin down Breaks,

NO SUNDAY TRAINS.

CROSSING ARRANGEMENTS.

Wyesham Junction and Tintern are the only intermediate Crossing Stations.

No. 4 Up Passenger to pass No. 3 Up Goods at Tintern.

No. 3 Up Goods to cross Nos. 4 and 5 Passenger Trains at Wyesham Junction.

No. 6 Down Goods to cross No. 7 Up Passenger at Tintern.

Working Timetable for March 1884

BANK HOLIDAY, WHIT MONDAY, JUNE, 10th

SPECIAL TIMETABLE FOR THE WYE VALLEY RAILWAY

ASSUMING DATE 1889

DOWN TRAINS

STATIONS		1 Coleford Pass. a.m.	2 First B'ham Exc. a.m.	3 Second B'ham Exc. a.m.	4 Third B'ham Exc. a.m.	5 Fourth B'ham Exc. a.m.	6 Ordinary Pass. a.m.	7 Coleford Pass. a.m.	8 Wolverh'ton Exc. a.m.	9 Engine of First B'ham Exc.	10 Ordinary Pass. p.m.	11 Coleford Pass. p.m.	12 Special Pass. p.m.	13 Ordinary Pass. p.m.	14 Coleford Pass. p.m.	15 Ordinary Pass. p.m.	16 Ordinary Pass. p.m.
Monmouth	dep	8.3	8.5	8.15	8.29	8.44	9.0	9.20	9.26	—	12.25	12.50		3.43	4.45	6.0	—
Wyesham Junction	"	8.6	8.8	8.18	8.32	8.47	9.3	9.23	9.29	—	12.27	12.55		3.48	4.50	6.3	—
Redbrook	"						9.7				12.31			3.52		6.7	—
Bigsweir			8.28				9.15			12.5	12.38		4.0	4.9		6.15	
Tintern	arr			8.38	8.52	9.7	9.23		9.49		12.45		4.4	4.12		6.23	7.40
"	dep			8.43	8.55	9.10	9.25		9.55	12.14	12.47		4.11	4.21		6.26	7.50
Tidenham							9.35				12.56		4.14	4.24		6.37	
Wye Valley Junction	arr					9.25	9.38		10.10	12.17	12.59		4.17	4.27		6.40	7.53
Chepstow	arr			8.58	9.10	9.30	9.40		10.15		1.2		4.20	4.40		6.43	7.56
"	dep						9.42		10.18		1.3			4.45		6.45	8.0
Portskewett	arr			9.03	9.15	9.33	9.51		10.20		1.13		4.30			6.55	8.07
Severn Tunnel Junction	arr			9.06	9.18	9.45	9.56		10.30	12.20	1.18		4.35			7.0	8.12

CROSSING ARRANGEMENTS No. 10 down train to cross No. 5 up train at W.V. Jct. No. 15 down train to cross No. 9 up train at Tintern. No. 10 down train to cross No. 12 up train at W.V. Jct.

UP TRAINS

r.r. There trains will run if required only.

STATIONS		1 Ordinary Pass. a.m.	2 Coleford Pass. a.m.	3 Ordinary Pass. a.m.	4 Coleford Pass. p.m.	5 Engine of First B'ham Exc.	6 Coleford Pass. p.m.	7 Ordinary Pass. p.m.	8 Coleford Pass. p.m.	9 Ordinary Pass. p.m.	10 First B'ham Return Exc. p.m.	11 Ordinary Pass. p.m.	12 Second B'ham Return Exc. p.m.	13 Third B'ham Return Exc. p.m.	14 Fourth B'ham Return Exc. p.m.	15 Wolverh'ton Return Exc. p.m.
Severn Tunnel Junction	dep	7.05		10.30		12.55		2.30		5.45	6.20	7.0	7.50	8.3	7.55	8.25
Portskewett	arr	7.18		10.36		1.0		2.36		5.51	6.35	7.6	7.54	8.3	8.05	8.35
Chepstow	dep	7.19		10.45		1.3		2.45		6.0	6.50	7.15	8.10	8.23	8.15	8.45
Wye Valley Junction	arr	7.22		11.05		1.13		2.47		6.3	6.53	7.18	8.15	8.28	8.18	8.48
Tidenham	dep	7.25		11.08				2.50		6.9						
Tintern	arr	7.34		11.11				2.53		6.19	7.15	7.25	8.32	8.47	8.38	9.08
"	dep	7.36		11.21				3.5		6.24	7.25				8.43	9.13
Bigsweir		7.43		11.31				3.14		6.33						
Redbrook		7.53		11.41				3.24		6.43						
Wyesham Junction		7.56	8.47	11.44	12.07		2.30	3.27	5.47	6.47	7.47				9.02	9.32
Monmouth	arr	7.58	8.50	11.47	12.10		2.35	3.30	5.50	6.50	7.50	7.33	8.35	8.50	9.05	9.35

WYE VALLEY RAILWAY.   Single Line.   (No Sunday Trains.)

DOWN TRAINS.

STATIONS.	Gradient 1 in	Point to Point Times.	Allow for Stop.	Allow for Start.	1 B Coleford Pass. dep.	2 Passenger. arr.	2 Passenger. dep.	8 B Coleford Pass. dep.	8 Passenger. arr.	8 Passenger. dep.	Coleford Mixed Train. arr.	Coleford Mixed Train. dep.	Goods. S.T. 522. arr.	Goods. S.T. 522. dep.	Passenger. arr.	Passenger. dep.	Coleford Mixed Train. arr.	Coleford Mixed Train. dep.	9 B Passenger. arr.	9 B Passenger. dep.
		Mins.	Mins.	Mins.	A.M.	A.M.	A.M.	A.M.	A.M.	A.M.	P.M.	P.M.	P.M.	P.M.	P.M.	P.M.	P.M.	P.M.	P.M.	P.M.
Monmouth (Troy)	66 R	3	1	1	8 ·	8 40	8 59	9 40		12 17		12 55	1 20X	1 15		2 0		4 0		5 57
Wysham Junct.	80 F	4	1	1									1 35	1 30						5 59
Redbrook	132 R	8	1	1		9 17	9 3	9 43	12 28	11 19			2 10	2 0		4 6		4 14		6 3
St. Briavels & Llandogo	80 R	8	1	1			9 11		12 31	11 30			2 36X	2 25		4 14		4 23		6 11
Tintera (for Brockweir)							9 18		X12 33							4 20			6 17	6 21
Wire Works Junction	80 F																			
Tidenham	66 F	15	1	1		9 32	9 27	9 37	12 47				3 40	3 45	4 31	4 34		4 42	6 29	6 31
Wye Valley Junction	66 F	3	1	1			9 30		12 30				3 55	3 50	4 39	4 37		4 51	X	6 37
Chepstow							9 37		12 52	1 37				5 0	4 57					6 46
Portskewett							9 46						6 25	6 25					6 52	
Severn Tunnel Junc.					9 52			1 42												

UP TRAINS.

STATIONS.	Gradient 1 in	Point to Point Times.	Allow for Stop.	Allow for Start.	1 B Passenger. arr.	1 B Passenger. dep.	3 B Coleford Pass. arr.	Goods. S.T. 523. arr.	Goods. S.T. 523. dep.	Passenger. arr.	Passenger. dep.	Coleford Mixed Train. arr.	Coleford Mixed Train. dep.	Passenger. arr.	Passenger. dep.	Coleford Passenger. arr.	Coleford Passenger. dep.	Passenger. arr.	Passenger. dep.
		Mins.	Mins.	Mins.	A.M.	A.M.	A.M.	A.M.	A.M.	A.M.	A.M.	P.M.	P.M.	P.M.	P.M.	P.M.	P.M.	P.M.	P.M.
Severn Tunnel Junc.						6 50		10 50	10 40	11 12	11 45	11 19			2 30			6 21	
Portskewett	266 R							10 55	11 0		11 28	11 30		2 45	2 37			6 28	
Chepstow	66 R	2	1		7 2	7 9		11 0	11 0		11 36				2 54			6 36	6 38
Wye Valley Junction	95 F		1		7 11	7 16												X	6 44
Tidenham	80 F	11	1		7 23	7 25		11 15	X12 45	X11 49	11 46			3 0	3 3			6 52	6 54
Wire Works Junction	179 R	8	1			7 32		12 55	12 55		11 53				3 11			7	7 10
Tintera (for Brockweir)	211 R	10	1		7 39	7 41		1 12	1 0	12 0	12 2			3 18	3 20			7	7 13
St. Briavels & Llandogo	80 R	6	1			7 14				12 55									
Redbrook	66 F	2	1			7 46		1 35	X130	1 25	12 7			3 23	3 25		5 47	7 15	
Wysham Junct.							8 42							2 43		5 44			
Monmouth (Troy)							8 45	11 56		12 7	12 2		2 45						

Single Line between Monmouth (Troy) and Wye Valley Junction worked by Electric Train Staff.

The Intermediate Crossing Stations are TINTERN and WYESHAM JUNCTION.

W This Train will be banked to Wyesham Junction when necessary, but the load must not exceed 35 Wagons.

Working Timetable for April 1910

Name of Place.	From	To	Miles per hour
CHEPSTOW AND MONMOUTH.			
Wye Valley Junction	Main Line	Wye Valley Line and vice versa	10
Tintern Station	{ Chepstow	Monmouth	10
	{ Monmouth	Chepstow	10
Between Monmouth (Troy) and Redbrook 13m. 46ch. and 13m. 39ch.	Monmouth	Chepstow and vice versa ..	20

Maximum Loads for Main Line Freight Trains

SECTION. From	To	WORKING LOADS. Maximum number of wagons to be conveyed except by Trains specially provided for in the Service Books or by arrangement.	For Group **A** Engines.				For Group **B** Engines.				For Group **C** Engines.			
			Class 1 Traffic.	Class 2 Traffic.	Class 3 Traffic.	Empties.	Class 1 Traffic.	Class 2 Traffic.	Class 3 Traffic.	Empties.	Class 1 Traffic.	Class 2 Traffic.	Class 3 Traffic. Y	Empties.
UP.														
Chepstow . ..	Tintern	50	15	18	23	30	17	20	26	34	19	23	29	38
Tintern	Redbrook ..	50	26	31	39	52	30	36	45	60	32	38	48	64
Redbrook.. ..	Monmouth Troy	50	18	22	27	36	21	25	32	42	22	26	33	44
DOWN.														
Monmouth Troy	Redbrook ..	50	15	18	23	30	17	20	26	34	19	23	29	38
Redbrook ..	Tintern	50	36	43	54	60	42	50	63	80	45	54	68	85
Tintern	Chepstow ..	50	18	22	27	36	21	25	32	42	22	26	33	44

STANDARD LOADS OF PASSENGER, PARCELS AND FISH TRAINS FOR ENGINE WORKING PURPOSES.

SECTION.		CLASS OF ENGINE.					
FROM	TO	3300-3455 4400 4410 4500-4599 5500-5574 57, 77, 87 & 97XX	3252-3291 1003-1013 2251-2280 0-6-2 T "B" Group—	0-6-0 & 0-6-0 T. 0-6-2 T. A Group.	3210 to 3225 1119-1128	2-4-0 T. Metro 0-4-2T. 48 & 58XX 898 900 908 910	0-4-2 T (517 Class) 1334 1335 1336
		Tons	Tons	Tons	Tons	Tons	Tons
Monmouth ..	Ross ..	310	—	260	260	220	200
Ross .. .	Monmouth ..	310	—	260	260	220	200
Chepstow ..	Tintern ..	225	—	175 200§	—	140	120
Tintern ..	Monmouth ..	225	—	175 200§	—	160	140
Monmouth ..	Pontypool Road	240 249§	—	190 224§	—	170	150

Extracts from Appendix to Working Timetables

WYE VALLEY BRANCH.

Motor Trolley System of Maintenance.

1. This system of maintenance operates from 0 miles 2 chains Wye Valley Junction, to 13 miles 66 chains Monmouth (Troy) and the Standard Instructions relating to the Motor Trolley System of Maintenance shewn on pages 65–68 of the General Appendix to the Rule Book, together with the following special instructions, will apply.

2. The undermentioned engineering gangs will be responsible for that Section of the line :—

No.	Home Station.	m.	ch.	m.	ch.
111	St. Briavels	0	2	11	46
71	Monmouth (Troy)	11	46	13	66

3. Occupation key instruments and telephones are installed at Boxes situated at the mileage given below, and in the undermentioned Signal Boxes :—

Section—Wye Valley Junction to Tintern.

(One key.) Gang No. 111. 0 miles, 2 chains, to 4 miles 51 chains.

	m.	ch.
Wye Valley Junction Signal Box	0	0
Tidenham Ground Frame	0	70
Box No. 1	1	31
Box No. 2	2	12†
Box No. 3	3	0
Box No. 4	3	65
Tintern Signal Box	4	51

The telephones communicate with the Signalman at Wye Valley Junction and Tintern.

† This box also contains an additional instrument for the blasting key (see instructions on page 76).

Section—Tintern to Monmouth (Troy).

Group A. (One key.) Gang No. 111. 4 miles 51 chains, to 11 miles 46 chains.

Group B. (One key.) Gang No. 71. 11 miles 46 chains, to 13 miles 66 chains.

Group A.

	m.	ch.
Tintern Signal Box	4	51
Box No. 5	5	35
Box No. 6	6	26
Box No. 7	7	11
St. Briavels Ground Frame	8	4
Box No. 8	8	56
Box No. 9	9	35
Box No. 10	10	15
Box No. 11	10	70
Redbrook Ground Frame	11	46

Group B.

	m.	ch.
Redbrook Ground Frame	11	46
Box No. 12	12	32
Box No. 13	13	8
Monmouth (Troy) Signal Box	13	66

The telephones communicate with the Signalman at Monmouth (Troy).

4. Control instruments are provided in the Section between Tintern and Monmouth (Troy).

5. When occupation keys for groups 'A' and 'B' have been withdrawn simultaneously, the Ganger who restores the occupation key first must remain at the box where the occupation key has been replaced, until informed by the Signalman at Monmouth (Troy) that the electric train staff instruments have been tested, and that everything is in order.

6. Before closing the Signal Box each night, the Signalman must place the occupation key in the box provided for the purpose outside his Signal Box, in order that the key for each respective group may be available for the use of the Ganger for the inspection of the line on Sundays—when required, and at any other time when it may be considered necessary, or desirable, to do so. The keys will be placed in the boxes by the Signalman as under :—

Signal Box.	Section for which occupation key must be withdrawn.
Tintern	Tintern and Wye Valley Junction.
Monmouth (Troy)	Monmouth (Troy) to Redbrook portion of Monmouth (Troy) and Tintern Section.

After the last train has cleared the Section, the person in charge at St. Briavels must, in conjunction with the Signalmen at Tintern and Monmouth (Troy) and in accordance with the standard instructions, withdraw each night the occupation key, and place it in the box provided for the purpose, to be available for use by the Ganger the next morning.

7. An Annett's key is attached to the respective occupation keys at Redbrook, St. Briavels, and Tidenham, to enable the Ganger to enter the Sidings with the motor trolleys when required.

When the Ganger requires to use the Siding points at Redbrook, St. Briavels, or Tidenham, he must insert the Annett's key attached to the occupation key, in the Ground Frame. After unlocking the Ground Frame and opening the Siding points, the Annett's key cannot be removed until the points have been placed in the proper position for trains to pass upon the Running line, and securely locked so as to prevent vehicles passing from the Sidings on to the Running line.

Extracts from the 1943 Working Appendix

Wye Valley Branch—*continued.*

Working of Tender Engines.

Tender engines must not run over the Wye Valley Branch with tender first.

TINTERN (FOR BROCKWEIR.)

To prevent vehicles running away towards Monmouth from the loop line at Tintern, a catchpoint is fixed at the North end of the loop, and no Passenger train must be started out of the loop towards Monmouth.

The loop, however, may be used for excursion and other trains starting towards Chepstow.

Tintern Quarries.

The Quarry Siding is situated between Tintern and Wye Valley Junction on the Down side of the line, and the connection to the single line is worked by a two lever Ground Frame, known as Tintern Quarries North Ground Frame.

The points in the single line, which are facing to a train running from Tintern to Wye Valley Junction, are worked and bolt locked from the Ground Frame, the latter being locked by a key on the electric train staff.

When an Up Freight train is working at the Ground Frame, the train or vehicles left on the single line must be secured in accordance with Rule 151.

Blasting operations will be arranged at the Quarry in the early morning prior to the passing of the first train over the line, and the necessary arrangements must be made between the Firm and the Tintern Station Master the previous day.

A special occupation key box, fitted with a separate key lettered "Permission to blast" is provided in the occupation hut adjacent to the quarry for use in connection with blasting operations.

The Standard Instructions for Occupation of Branch Lines by the Permanent Way Department under the Motor Trolley System of Maintenance of Branch Lines shewn on pages 65 68 of the General Appendix to the Rule Book, will apply in regard to the special key provided for blasting purposes, except that it must only be withdrawn or replaced in the key box provided.

The key cannot be withdrawn when the occupation key for No. 1 group, *viz.*, Wye Valley Junction to Tintern, has been withdrawn.

The Station Master must arrange for the Tidenham Goods Porter to attend at the site for the purpose of withdrawing and replacing the special key when blasting operations are required. The Tintern Station Signal Box must be opened earlier to enable the key to be withdrawn. The key must be replaced in the key box by 7.30 a.m.

After the blasting operations are completed, the man in charge of the special blasting key must comply with Clause 7 (Sections *e* and *f*) of the Standard Instructions for Occupation of Branch Lines (pages 65 68 of the General Appendix to the Rule Book) and in the event of any obstruction of the line through falling debris or otherwise, Clause 8 of the instructions must be immediately carried out.

IMPORTANT DATES AND EVENTS

1865	First plans of proposed railway drawn up.
13th July, 1866	Reading of Parliamentary Bill (amended plan).
10th August, 1866	Parliamentary sanctions line.
22nd November, 1872	Formal agreement signed for the building of Wireworks branch.
25th March, 1874	Publication of prospectus.
May, 1874	Construction work commences on Wye Valley line.
June, 1874	Construction work commences on Wireworks branch.
August, 1874	Wireworks branch completed.
14th June, 1875	Wye Valley Railway Amendment Act passed.
28th October, 1876	Special train carrying officials makes journey along branch.
1st November, 1876	Railway officially opened to the public.
1st September, 1883	Wyesham Junction to Coleford branch opened.
December, 1904	Circular from Chairman to Shareholders informing them of takeover.
1st July, 1905	Wye Valley Railway amalgamated with the G.W.R.
1st May, 1909	Bigsweir station renamed St. Briavels and Llandogo.
1912	Tintern station renamed Tintern for Brockweir.
1st January, 1917	Coleford branch closed.
January, 1917	Tidenham station closed.
1st February, 1918	Tidenham station re-opened.
1st February, 1927	The appendage Llandogo dropped from St. Briavels station.
1st February, 1927	Whitebrook Halt opened.
11th January, 1927	Redbrook signal box closed.
7th March, 1927	Llandogo Halt opened.
21st November, 1928	St. Briavels signal box closed.
30th October, 1928	Tidenham signal box closed.
July, 1929	Remaining sections of Coleford Branch removed.
23rd September, 1929	Brockweir Halt opened.
12th January, 1931	Wyesham Halt opened.
1st August, 1931	Penallt Halt opened.
18th July, 1932	Netherhope Halt opened.
1935	Redbrook station renamed Redbrook-on-Wye.
February, 1941	Rails lifted on Wireworks Branch.
4th January, 1959	Last passenger train to use the Wye Valley line.
5th January, 1959	Line officially closed to passenger traffic.
6th January, 1964	Line closed completely from Monmouth Troy station to Tintern Quarry.
24th August, 1964	Tintern Branch worked as private siding.

Acknowledgement: I would like to add a thank you to Mr. W. A. Camwell and Mr. M. Lines for their co-operation and assistance with the project—B.M.H.

GRADIENTS SHOWN ON WYE VALLEY RAILWAY PLANS

The information is dated 1875, Gwent County Council Records No. P & BR 419. Wye Valley Junction being zero miles and chains. Total length given as 13 miles 2 furlongs 9 chains 75 links to Wyesham Junction.

0—10 ch. Level.
10 to 45 ch. 1 : 66 up.
45 ch. to 2 miles level, including 995 yd. tunnel (Tidenham).
2 miles to 2 ml. 73 ch. 1 : 100 down.
2 ml. 73 ch. to 3 ml. 40 ch. Level.
3 ml. 40 ch. to 4 ml. 1 : 100 down.
4 ml. to 4 ml. 16 ch. 1 : 100 down.
4 ml. 16 ch. to 4 ml. 25 ch. Level including 165 yd. tunnel (Tintern) 2nd. 64 yd. bridge.
4 ml. 25 ch. to 5 ml. 1 : 100 down.
5 ml. to 6 ml. Level.
6 ml. to 6 ml. 35 ch. 1 : 170 up.
6 ml. 35 ch. to 6 ml. 70 ch. 1 : 211 down.
6 ml. 70 ch. to 7 ml. 5 ch. 1 : 211 up.
7 ml. 5 ch. to 7 ml. 35 ch. 1 : 638 down.
7 ml. 35 ch. to 8 ml. Level.
8 ml. to 8 ml. 5 ch. Level.
8 ml. 5 ch. to 8 ml. 45 ch. 1 : 122 up.
8 ml. 45 ch. to 9 ml. 15 ch. 1 : 390 up.
9 ml. 15 ch. to 9 ml. 30 ch. Level.
9 ml. 30 ch. to 9 ml. 60 ch. 1 : 255 up.
9 ml. 60 ch. to 10 ml. 1 : 132 up.
10 ml. to 10 ml. 10 ch. 1 : 132 up.
10 ml. to 10 ml. 15 ch. Level.
10 ml. 15 ch. to 10 ml. 55 ch. 1 : 211 down.
10 ml. 55 ch. to 10 ml. 75 ch. 1 : 200 up
10 ml. 75 ch. to 11 ml. 16 ch. 1 : 200 up
11 ml. 16 ch. to 11 ml. 33 ch. 1 : 200 up
11ml. 33 ch. to 11 ml. 45 ch. Level including bridge.
11 ml. 45 ch. to 12 ml. 1 : 80 up.
12 ml. 45 ch. to 13 ml. 5 ch. Level.
13 ml. 5 ch. to 13 ml. 29 ch. 1 : 77 down Wyesham.

STATION PLANS

The following plans are of the four orginal stations that were built by the Wye Valley Railway Co. during the construction of the line.

The only major changes that occurred to the stations during their lifetime was the closure of individual signal boxes, consequently control of loops and sidings were given over to ground frame levers. The following list gives dates and details of signal box closures. The plans are not to scale.

REDBROOK-ON-WYE

From the 30th September, 1925 the signal box was only manned as required, it was closed altogether in January, 1927 the loop being controlled by ground frame levers.

BIGSWEIR

This signal box was closed altogether in the latter part of November, 1928. Sidings and loop being controlled by ground frame levers.

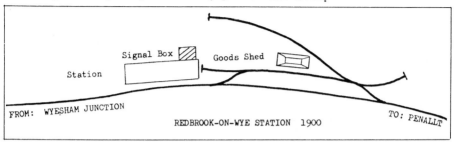

Signal Box · Goods Shed · Station
FROM: WYESHAM JUNCTION
TO: PENALLT

REDBROOK-ON-WYE STATION 1900

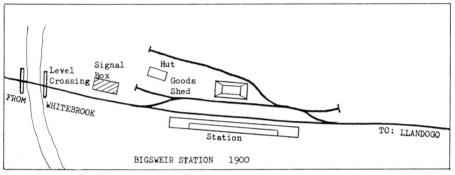

Level Crossing · Signal Box · Hut · Goods Shed · Station
FROM WHITEBROOK
TO: LLANDOGO

BIGSWEIR STATION 1900

TIDENHAM

When Tidenham Station first opened the complex comprised of a platform and station buildings, signal box and a goods shed. The track layout consisted of a loop which ran parallel to the station and a short spur siding that served the goods shed. This arrangement remained for half a century, until the closure of the signal box in the autumn of 1928. Control of the loop and siding was then given over to ground frame levers positioned north and south of the loop. The last major alteration at Tidenham during the railway's working life happened in the Winter of 1952 when the loop and consequently the south ground frame were taken out of use. The north frame and goods siding remained until February, 1955 when it too was abandoned. The station ended its days having been demoted to the status of a halt. The buildings, signal box and goods shed were demolished soon after closure as the site was taken over by quarry contractors who developed the original platform into a loading bay for locally quarried ballast stone. In March, 1968 a new loop again running parallel to the platform and two new ground frames were laid in order to provide a runaround for the ballast trains.

TINTERN

The largest railway complex on the branch. The development consisted of main station buildings, goods shed, cattle psns, loading bays, signal box and an island platform that provided shelter for trains starting for Chepstow but not for Monmouth. Movement on the loops was controlled by siding signals positioned at either end. The signal box was closed on the 6th January, 1964. The main station building and signal box escaped total destruction; the structures were renovated and are now open to the public as a picnic area.

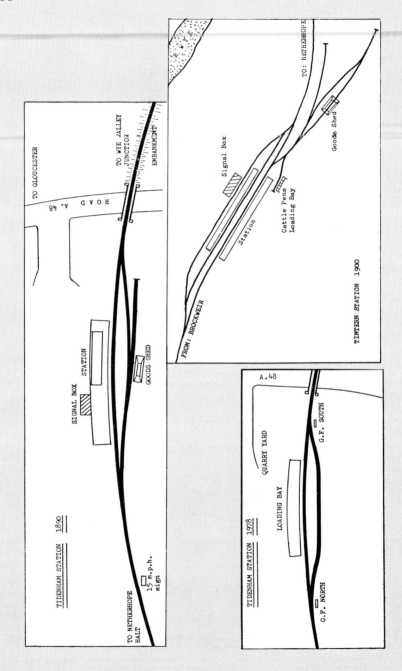

TIDENHAM STATION 1890

TO GLOUCESTER

ROAD A.48

TO WYE VALLEY JUNCTION

EMBANKMENT

SIGNAL BOX

STATION

GOODS SHED

TO NETHERHOPE HALT

15 m.p.h. sign

TIMTERN STATION 1900

FROM: BROCKWEIR

R W Y E

Signal Box

Station

Cattle Pens
Loading Bay

Goods Shed

TO: NETHERHOPE

TIDENHAM STATION 1978

A.48

QUARRY YARD

LOADING BAY

G.F. NORTH

G.F. SOUTH

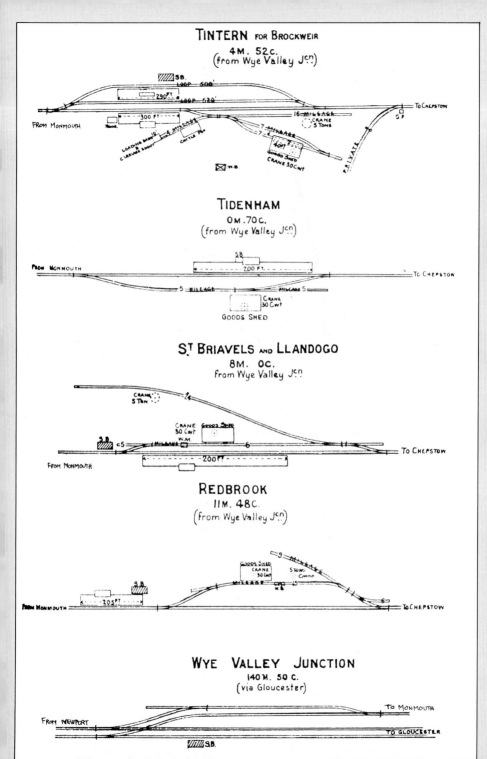

TINTERN FOR BROCKWEIR
4M. 52C.
(from Wye Valley Jcn.)

TIDENHAM
0M. 70C.
(from Wye Valley Jcn.)

ST BRIAVELS AND LLANDOGO
8M. 0C.
from Wye Valley Jcn.

REDBROOK
11M. 48C.
(from Wye Valley Jcn.)

WYE VALLEY JUNCTION
140M. 50C.
(via Gloucester)

EACH WEEK-DAY

G.W.R. Circular Tour from Gloucester through the

BEAUTIFUL WYE VALLEY

enabling passengers to visit

Ross-on-Wye, Symonds Yat, Monmouth, Tintern or Chepstow

CHEAP DAY CIRCULAR TOUR TICKETS are issued from GLOUCESTER

RETURN FARE **5/0** THIRD CLASS

Passengers may travel on the forward journey via Ross-on-Wye and Monmouth, returning via Chepstow and Grange Court; or forward via Grange Court and Chepstow, returning via Monmouth and Ross-on-Wye. They may also break their journey at Chepstow, Tintern, St. Briavels, Llandogo, Redbrook-on-Wye, Monmouth, Symonds Yat, or Ross-on-Wye, but must return to Gloucester the same day.

THREE WYE VALLEY Circular Tours by G.W.R. from NEWPORT

RETURN FARES 3rd class

The following is an Itinerary of each Tour:—

TOUR No. 1.—Raglan, Monmouth, Tintern, Chepstow. Passengers travel to Tintern either via Chepstow or via Pontypool Road and Monmouth, and are entitled to break the journey either going or returning at Raglan, Monmouth, Redbrook-on-Wye, St. Briavels, Tintern, or Chepstow, and to travel to and fro by either route . **3s. 8d.**

TOUR No. 2.—Usk, Monmouth, Symonds Yat, Chepstow. Passengers travel to Symonds Yat either via Chepstow and Monmouth, or v a Pontypool Road and Monmouth, and may break their journey either going or returning at Usk, Raglan, Monmouth, Redbrook-on-Wye, St. Briavels, Tin ern or Chepstow, enabling them to travel to or fro by either route . **4s. 6d.**

TOUR No. 3.—Monmouth, Symonds Yat, Ross-on-Wye, Chepstow. Passengers travel to Ross-on-Wye either via Chepstow and Monmouth or via Pontypool Road and Monmouth, and may break their journey either going or returning at Usk, Raglan, Monmouth, Redbrook-on-Wye, St. Briavels, Tintern, Chepstow, Symonds Yat, or Kerne Bridge, enabling them to travel to or fro by either route . **5s. 6d.**

For further details see handbills obtainable at local stations.

G.W.R. CHEAP DAY FARES FOR RAMBLERS.

FROM	To Newport 1st.	3rd.	To Abergavenny 1st.	3rd.	To Hereford 1st.	3rd.	To Ross-on-Wye 1st.	3rd.	To Symonds Yat 1st.	3rd.	To M'nm'th Troy 1st.	3rd.	To M'nm'th May Hill 1st.	3rd.	To Lydney 1st.	3rd.	To Usk 1st.	3rd.	To Tintern 1st.	3rd.	To Chepstow 1st.	3rd.	To Gloucester 1st.	3rd.	To Pontypool Rd. 1st.	3rd.	To Raglan 1st.	3rd.
	s. d.	s. d.	s. d.	s. d.	s. d.	s. d.	s. d.	s. d.	s. d.	s. d.	s. d.	s. d.	s. d.	s. d.	s. d.	s. d.	s. d.	s. d.	s. d.	s. d.	s. d.	s. d.	s. d.	s. d.	s. d.	s. d.	s. d.	s. d.
ABERDARE (high l.)	5 11	3 11	6 3	4 2	11 2	7 5	—	—	—	—	—	—	—	—	—	—	—	—	—	—	—	—	—	—	4 9	3 2	—	—
ABERGAVENNY	4 0	2 8	—	—	4 9	3 2	7 2	4 9	6 3	4 2	5 2	3 5	—	—	—	—	2 8	1 9	—	—	—	—	2 0	1 4	4 0	2 8	—	—
ABERTILLERY	3 5	2 3	2 0	1 10	—	—	7 2	4 9	5 11	3 11	—	—	—	—	—	—	—	—	7 11	5 3	7 2	4 9	—	—	4 9	3 2	—	—
BLAENAVON	3 0	2 0	3 6	2 4	7 6	5 0	7 11	5 3	6 3	4 2	5 6	3 8	2 9	1 10	—	—	—	—	—	—	—	—	—	—	4 0	2 8	—	—
CHELTENHAM (S. J.)	—	—	—	—	7 6	5 0	4 11	3 3	6 9	4 6	—	—	7 6	5 0	5 6	3 8	—	—	7 11	5 3	7 2	4 9	—	—	—	—	—	—
CHEPSTOW	3 6	2 4	—	—	5 6	3 8	4 5	2 11	3 2	2 1	—	—	—	—	1 3	9½	—	—	—	—	—	—	5 6	3 8	—	—	4 5	2 11
EBBW VALE	4 5	2 11	—	—	7 11	5 3	6 9	4 6	—	—	—	—	—	—	—	—	8 8	5 9	7 11	5 3	—	—	—	—	5 6	3 8	—	—
GLOUCESTER	—	—	—	—	6 0	4 0	3 6	2 4	5 2	3 5	—	—	6 0	4 0	4 0	2 8	—	—	6 3	4 2	5 6	3 8	—	—	—	—	—	—
HENGOED (high l.)	—	—	4 5	2 11	9 0	6 0	8 3	5 6	7 2	4 9	5 11	3 11	—	—	—	—	3 6	2 4	—	—	—	—	2 5	1 7	4 9	3 2	—	—
MONMOUTH (Troy)	5 6	3 8	5 2	3 5	5 2	3 5	2 9	1 10	1 3	9½	—	—	—	—	2 6	1 8	2 0	1 4	3 0	2 0	6 3	4 2	3 6	2 4	1 5	1 11	—	—
NEWNHAM	—	—	—	—	2 9	1 10	—	—	—	—	2 0	1 4	—	—	3 6	2 4	—	—	—	—	—	—	—	—	—	—	—	—
NEWPORT	—	—	4 0	2 8	8 8	5 9	8 5	5 6	6 9	4 6	5 6	3 8	—	—	2 10	1 11	4 9	3 2	3 6	2 4	9 0	6 0	1 8	1	4 2	2 9	—	—
PONTYPOOL ROAD	1 8	1	2 0	1	4 6	9 4	6 6	3 4	2 4	9 3	2 3	6 2	4	—	—	1 3	9½	—	—	—	—	—	—	2 5	1 7	—	—
RISCA	1 5	1 11	—	—	7 11	5 3	7 2	4 9	—	—	—	—	5 11	3 11	—	—	5 11	3 11	4 9	3 2	—	—	—	—	5 2	3 5	—	—
ROSS-ON-WYE	—	—	2 6	1 8	—	—	1 1	—	1 8	—	—	—	—	—	—	—	—	—	3 2	3 8	—	—	—	—	—	—	—	—
STROUD	—	—	8 5	5 7	5 11	3 11	5 0	—	—	—	—	—	6 3	4 2	8 8	5 9	7 11	5 3	—	—	—	—	—	—	—	—	—	—

c.—Via Brynmawr and L.M.S. Railway.

The above tickets are issued each weekday (and also on Sundays where train service is available) by any train.

NOTE.—For particulars of further Cheap Day Tickets from other Stations, see handbills and notices obtainable at Stations in the district concerned.